Northern Illinois
University

Center for
Southeast Asian
Studies

Monograph Series
on Southeast Asia

Ritual, Power, and Economy:
Upland-Lowland Contrasts in Mainland Southeast Asia

Susan D. Russell, Editor

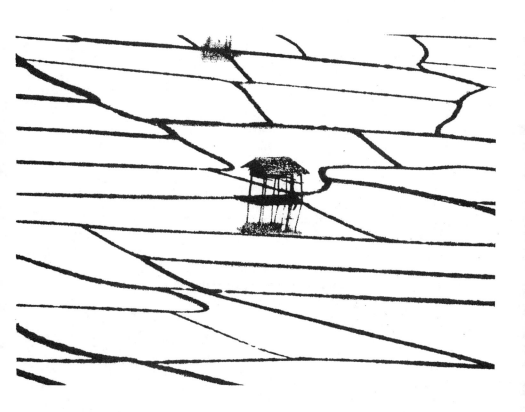

Occasional Paper No. 14, 1989

Center Director: Michael Aung-Thwin
Editor: Grant A. Olson
Copy Editor: David A. Mullikin

ISBN# 1-877979-14-7

RITUAL, POWER, AND ECONOMY:
Upland-Lowland Contrasts
in Mainland Southeast Asia

Edited by

Susan D. Russell

Editor's Foreword

Many of the papers in this volume were presented at the Southeast Asian Studies Summer Institute Conference at Northern Illinois University, DeKalb, Illinois, July 31-August 2, 1986. The title of the Symposium was "Ritual and Economic Change in the Southeast Asian Periphery."

I would like to express my appreciation to the Department of Anthropology at Northern Illinois University, especially Sue Dewey and Kathleen Truman for their typing assistance in the preparation of this monograph. I would also like to thank Cathy Bird for help in proofreading earlier drafts of these papers and Grant Olson for his editorial assistance.

Susan D. Russell
Northern Illinois University

CONTENTS

INTRODUCTION:
TRANSFORMATIONS IN RITUAL AND ECONOMY IN
UPLAND AND LOWLAND SOUTHEAST ASIA

Mark R. Woodward and Susan D. Russell

The defining role that cosmology and religion have played in Southeast Asian political structures is a classic theme that has been widely addressed in both lowland state contexts (Heine-Geldern 1942; Tambiah 1976, 1977) and in upland regions of mainland Southeast Asia (Leach 1954; Kirsch 1973). Concepts of secular and sacred power vary greatly throughout the region but comprise a limited range of permutations when viewed from their common interdependency with ritually enacted or prescribed validations of status. Ritual expressions of status and power, while derived from underlying religious cosmologies, constitute distinct systems of meaning that are formed in interaction with the changing forces of economy—an aspect that has been less often addressed in the literature. The papers in this volume explore the interdependence of cosmology, economy, status, and power in the animistic and Theravada Buddhist ritual traditions of mainland Southeast Asia. Each is a detailed ethnographic or historical case study of a particular tradition. Theoretically, they also contribute to the ongoing discourse in anthropology concerning the role that material phenomena and culture play in determining social organization and behavior. In mainland Southeast Asia, the analysis of ritual provides an entrée into the fundamental issues involved in this debate because it is the locus of significant (in materialistic terms) economic activity and is, at the same time, a matter of ultimate religious concern.

An enduring problem in the analysis of mainland Southeast Asian societies can be posed as a question: What is the proper way to view relationships between the religious beliefs of the lowlands, given the historical pre-eminence of Theravada Buddhist religious and political traditions, and those of upland animistic societies? This issue has been a problematic one ever since earlier, colonial notions of Buddhist belief and practice—largely derived from religious texts and scriptures—became increasingly untenable as empirical analyses documented local variations in Buddhist practices and the assimilation (and co-existence) of animistic beings and ideas in ritual performance and language. The "two religions" perspective in recent years has given way to new approaches that attempt to historically examine the development of Buddhism and animism within a single analytic framework. In the search for new ways to grapple with the disparities between religious texts and local belief systems and practices, anthropologists also have sought to incorporate the politico-economic role that external forces of markets and state play in the construction and constitution of cultural processes.

These basic issues form a common framework for the cases discussed in this volume. The papers also contribute to a major issue in the history and comparative ethnology of the region: the role of external political and economic factors in the construction of egalitarian or hierarchical systems of political authority. As Tambiah (1977), following Heine-Geldern (1942), has observed, the cosmology of early Southeast Asian states provides the "impulsion" for politics to be the enactment of ritual. In the uplands, too, as the different ideas of Leach (1954), Kirsch (1973), and Friedman (1979) exemplify, ritual as a means of displaying wealth and acquiring or validating status and power is intimately related to our understanding of the causes of variation and oscillation between egalitarian and hierarchic political systems. Our purpose in the remainder of this introduction is to present an overview of the background to these issues that will enable readers to place the individual contributions in broader theoretical, religious, and historical contexts.

Mainland Southeast Asia is an area of great geographic, cultural, and linguistic diversity. There are hundreds of ethno-linguistic groups and a wide variety of subsistence systems, modes of political organization, and religious traditions. A general distinction may be drawn between the upland cultures and those of the valleys and coasts. Upland societies are traditionally animistic and are based largely on swidden cultivation. Lowland states are primarily Theravada Buddhist and are based on wet rice cultivation.

The differences between upland animism and the Theravada Buddhism of the lowlands are enormous, including radically opposed cosmological, eschatological, and ethical systems, as well as distinct ritual traditions and concepts of causality. The contrast between upland and Buddhist views of killing and its place in ritual provides a particularly cogent example. In upland religions, the ritual slaughter of animals and the distribution of their flesh are the principle means through which humans acquire fertility, power, and status in the afterlife. Formerly, headhunting was undertaken in the hope that victims would contribute to the fertility and power of the village and become the slaves of their captor in the afterlife. In animistic traditions, therefore, death is the means through which religious ambitions are attained.

Nothing could be more different from the Theravada Buddhist prohibition of killing. The Pali scriptures mention abstention from killing as being among the cardinal virtues required of lay Buddhists (Lester 1973: 58-59). Theravada Buddhists view killing as an especially heinous sin that has significant eschatological consequences. What an upland feast-giver regards as the source of earthly prosperity and a happy afterlife is seen by Theravada Buddhism as the cause of a distinctly unpleasant rebirth that may last as long as one billion, six hundred and twenty million, million years (Reynolds and Reynolds 1982: 66).

2

In Burma, the consequences of killing and other sins are prominent themes in Buddhist art and exert a powerful influence on economic behavior and the interpretation of non-Buddhist religions. While most Burmese are not vegetarians, they take the prohibition against killing very seriously. Most are reluctant to use or sell rat poison, pesticides, and similar products. While these may be purchased openly in many markets, they are generally sold by Chinese, Christians, or Muslims. There are almost no Buddhist butchers. In Mandalay, the largest city in northern Burma, this practice has resulted in a curious religious division of labor. Cattle and goats are slaughtered by Muslims and hogs by Chinese. The result, from a Buddhist perspective, is that the demerit (and time in hell) resulting from slaughter falls on these individuals.

Despite these differences, upland and lowland cultures do not exist in isolation from one another. They are bound together by political, economic, and at times military ties. Leach (1954) and Lehman (1963, 1977) have shown that many upland societies are defined in terms of systematic and lasting relationships with lowland civilizations—so much so that origin myths often describe upland groups as ancestors and lowland peoples as brothers. The religious and ethical systems of some upland societies have also been influenced by the Theravada Buddhist concept of causality (Lehman 1977).

Lowland states have often used hill peoples as buffers against their neighbors, symbolically incorporating them as subordinate "states" in what Tambiah (1976) terms "galactic polities." Similarly, upland myths often claim that lowland kings have sought refuge in the hills during times of political instability. Moreover, despite the deep commitment of lowland peoples to Theravada Buddhism, there are also religious similarities. State cults and popular religion incorporate local spirits into Hindu and Buddhist pantheons. Like upland religions, such cults also are concerned with agricultural fertility and magical power. Both the Pali scriptures (Lester 1973: 60-61) and Southeast Asian Buddhist commentaries (Ledi Sayadaw 1965: 225; Reynolds and Reynolds 1982: 152-153) hold that the attainment of wealth is the consequence of moral action and that the ritual expenditure of wealth, primarily through gifts to the order of monks and to spiritual beings, are among the sources of earthly prosperity and future birth in heaven.

A number of historical and theoretical questions arise from these apparent similarities. One such question is the degree to which Theravada Buddhism, as practiced in contemporary Southeast Asia, retains the religious concerns and goals of indigenous traditions. A related issue is that of structural dominance; is Buddhism interpreted in terms of local animism or are animistic concerns and practices systematically incorporated into Buddhist cosmological and social systems? While such issues have great implications for the analysis of Southeast Asian history and cultures, they are empirical questions that may be answered only

3

through detailed case studies based on the careful consideration of ethnographic and Buddhological sources. An equally interesting theoretical issue is how a shared set of material concerns such as fertility and the attainment of prosperity are viewed from the perspective of different systems of meaning. An important question is how these interpretations shape the ways in which Theravada Buddhists and upland animists respond to their respective environments.

In this volume, papers by O'Connor and Tannenbaum examine the interrelation of Thai and Shan Buddhism and upland notions of power and fertility. Lehman discusses the impact of inflation, much of it originating from contact with the lowlands, on the ritual and political systems of the Chin and Kachin of Burma. Durrenberger presents a study of ritual and economy among the Lisu, an egalitarian society of northern Thailand. Like Lehman, he stresses the role of relations with lowland peoples in upland political and economic systems. Woodward examines links between polity, ritual, and economy among the Ao Naga of Assam, pointing to the contradiction between the economic goals and consequences of ritual performance.

Theravada Buddhism and Animism

Theravada Buddhism is among the world's "great religions." It dates to at least the third century B.C. and claims to uphold the original teachings and practices of the Buddha. The scriptural tradition was codified in the closing years of the first century B.C. and has, except for the composition of numerous commentaries in both Pali and local languages, remained virtually unchanged (Reynolds and Clifford 1987: 470). The soteriological goal of Theravada Buddhism, as constituted in the scriptural tradition, is the attainment of *nibbana* (enlightenment). *Nibbana* is viewed as escape from the cycle of rebirth *(samsara)* and the extinction of consciousness. This goal is achieved by the cultivation of knowledge about the causes of existence and the practice of morality. Throughout its history, Theravada Buddhism has emphasized the principle of world renunciation and the monastic ideal. Ultimately, each individual is responsible for his or her own salvation and must suffer or enjoy the fruits of moral and immoral action *(kamma)*.

Older Buddhological and anthropological scholarship on the Theravada tradition was *nibbana*-centric. It presumed that because enlightenment was the ultimate goal of the religion, all else was in some sense corrupt or even non-Buddhist. This orientation often led to the conclusion that aspects of religious belief and practice that were not explicitly focused on the attainment of enlightenment, particularly among the laity, were animistic or Hindu survivals. On the Buddhological side, this perspective may be traced to Rhys-Davids (1908) and others of the Pali Text Society, many of whom were personally committed to a *nibbana-*

4

centered Buddhism (see King 1964: 13) or to the study of Buddhism as a philosophical rather than cosmological or ritual order. Weber (1958: 192-230) based his sociological account of Buddhism on what is, by contemporary standards, a narrow reading of the textual tradition. He described early Buddhism as a religion of *nibbana*-oriented "cultured professional monks." He viewed the quest for *nibbana* as the religion of a cultivated, intellectual middle class (Weber 1958: 226) and felt that "authentic" Buddhism offered little for the masses. He described popular religion in Theravada societies as a combination of formulaic piety and belief in demons and magic (Weber 1958: 228). In short, Buddhism was seen as a thin veneer resting on top of an essentially animistic cosmology.

Among modern scholars, Spiro (1970) couples this interpretation with Freudian psychology. He argues that the cardinal doctrines of Theravada Buddhism, including *nibbana* and *anatta* (denial of the existence of a "self" or "soul"), are psychologically unacceptable and that popular religion is largely animistic. Such arguments have given rise to the "two religions" theory—the *nibbana*-oriented Buddhism of the (mostly monastic) minority and the syncretic Buddhism/Hinduism/animism of the masses.

Until recently, this perspective dominated discussions of Theravada Buddhism as practiced in mainland Southeast Asia and Sri Lanka. Opinion concerning the relative balance of Buddhist and other religious elements, however, remains sharply divided. In general, the stronger one's personal or intellectual commitment to the notion of an "authentic," purely soteriological, *nibbana*-focused interpretation of Buddhism, the more likely one is to view Buddhism as practiced in mainland Southeast Asia as "impure" or subordinate to some type of local animism.

Contemporary Buddhist reformists, for example, particularly those involved in lay meditation movements in Burma and Thailand, are quick to denounce as "non-Buddhist" spirit cults and other forms of religious practice that most Southeast Asians consider to be an integral part of their traditions. Scholarly proponents of this view maintain that "pure" Buddhism is the religion of a small minority and that most Southeast Asians are animists at heart. Bouquet (1961: 167) puts it this way: "...anyone who knows these countries is well aware that the real popular faith of their peoples is not Hinayana but a thinly veiled animism." Similar interpretations of Thai religion are found in the works of Boshe (1971) and Terwiel (1979). While Spiro (1967, 1970) emphasizes the importance of Theravada Buddhist concepts of *kamma* and rebirth, if not *nibbana* in Burmese religion, he clearly sees spirit cults as a distinct religious tradition.

The recent convergence of history of religions and cultural anthropological scholarship evident in the works of Keyes (1983, 1984), Lehman (1972, 1987), Tambiah (1970, 1976, 1984), Reynolds (1978a, 1972), and Schober (1980, 1984) has raised serious questions concerning the explanatory adequacy of any variant of the "two religions" theory. In general terms, anthropologists have become increasingly aware of the importance of the Theravada textual tradition in the lives of "ordinary" Buddhists, while Buddhological understanding of the textual tradition itself has become increasingly complex. As a discipline, the history of religions has shed much of its theological background and is increasingly concerned with non-soteriological aspects of religion and with the ways in which "great religions" are interpreted and enacted in varying local contexts. Concern with scriptural orthodoxy is rapidly giving way to fascination with the almost infinite variety of ways in which the central ideas of religious traditions give rise to local cults and social formations. Consequently, Theravada Buddhism is no longer understood as a purely soteriological religion. As Reynolds and Reynolds (1982: 5-41) observe, it is a complex tradition that, virtually from its inception, has included Buddhological, mythological, cosmological, and political as well as soteriological variants. Simply because a particular aspect of religious belief or practice is not directly geared to the attainment of enlightenment does not mean that it should not be considered Buddhist. Theravada Buddhism is a totalistic religion that explains not only the path to enlightenment, but also the nature and origins of the worldly context within which enlightenment must be sought.

Anthropological scholarship has approached many of the same issues, but from a slightly different perspective. In a review of Spiro's *Buddhism and Society: A Great Tradition and its Burmese Vicissitudes,* Lehman (1972) argues that the distinction between Buddhist and non-Buddhist cannot be based on the blind comparison of canonical texts and local religious practice. Rather, Buddhism must be understood as a set of principles or concepts that may be expressed in a multiplicity of textual, ritual, and social contexts and used to explain or impart meaning to diverse phenomena. Seen from this perspective, texts, which for Weber and others represented the "pure," "authentic" Buddhism, are only one expression of a set of underlying ideas or axioms that may also find expression in ritual, politics, and other aspects of social life.

In a subsequent study, Lehman (1987) demonstrates that while many Burmese spirits *(nat)* are directly associated with the Theravada textual tradition, others are of indigenous and even Muslim origin. But as a whole, human relationships with spirits are structured by Buddhist concepts. Guardian spirits are thought to establish social, economic, and political conditions within which Buddhism may flourish. Malevolent spirits, on the other hand, must be placated or controlled lest they interfere with the practice of Buddhism. In this respect, the organization of the Burmese *nat* cult and the Lao spirit cults described by Reynolds (1978b) mirror that of descriptions of spirits found in the Theravada textual tradition. Spirits are particularly important in narrative texts concerning the lives of the Buddha. In the *Jataka* narratives (describing the Buddha's former lives), Sakka (Sanskrit Indra), the king of the gods, regularly comes to the aid of the future Buddha, to the extent of advising him concerning the proper way to seek enlightenment (see Cowell 1957: 1-2). There are also all varieties of evil spirits, ogres, and mythological creatures that must be overcome (see Francis 1957: 2-13). Given these textual precedents, it is not surprising that "spirit cults" are important elements of lay Buddhism. As Reynolds (1978b: 170) points out, non-Buddhist spirits must be "tamed and drawn into the service of Buddhism." This situation presents practicing Buddhists with a paradox, because to control these beings it is sometimes necessary to employ means that are not in accord with Buddhist concepts of morality or do not make a direct contribution to the acquisition of merit or the attainment of enlightenment. Reynolds, for example, shows that in the Lao state cult pre-Buddhist ritual systems were required to control local spirits. Similarly, as Schober (personal communication) observes, some Burmese *nat* demand offerings of liquor in exchange for their assistance.

Theravada Buddhism's concern with the affairs of the world is not limited to spirit cults. Reynolds (1978b) observes that the textual tradition includes diverse models for social order ranging from the republicanism of the *Mahaparinibbana Sutta* to the concept of the *cakkavatti* (the world-conquering king). While *nibbana* and the path towards it are the ultimate concerns of the textual tradition, it also includes (*contra* Weber) a lay ethic centering on the eschatological, political, and economic consequences of moral behavior. While recent studies (such as Reynolds 1972; Smith 1978; Tambiah 1976) have emphasized Theravada Buddhist notions of kingship, the textual tradition also makes reference to economy, agricultural fertility, and power.

'Giving' (Pali, *dana*) is perhaps the cardinal virtue of lay Buddhism; the *sangha* (order of monks) depends entirely on lay donations for material support. In the *Questions of King Malinda*, it is explained that generosity is a "bridge" enabling lay people to progress on the path to enlightenment (Rhys-Davids 1890: 173-175). As Lester (1973: 59-52) points out, lay people are encouraged to acquire wealth by honest means and to use it for the support of religion. Ownership, debtlessness, and wealth are all described as types of bliss. Moreover, the *Sigolavada Sutta*, which is expressly concerned with lay conduct, warns against the needless dissipation of wealth. In a similar vein, the Buddha advised lay people to spend one part of their income, invest two, and save one for emergencies (Rhys Davids 1921: 168-184). While Theravada Buddhism forbids monks to possess money, it embraces the notion of well-gotten and well-used wealth for the lay supporters of religion.

The Theravada canon also includes discussions of the religious basis of agricultural fertility that are echoed in local cosmological texts and in popular mythology. *The Book of Gradual Sayings* (Woodward 1933, vol. 2: 85) states that when kings are righteous, the sky *deva* ("gods") will bestow sufficient rains. The relationship between kings, *deva*, and rain is expressed in the opposite fashion in Thai cosmological texts, where it is stated that if kings act wrongly the *deva* will prevent rain and ruin the crops (Reynolds and Reynolds 1982: 153). Tambiah's (1970: 165, 303-304) observation that northeastern Thai villagers make offerings to Buddhist saints, *deva*, and local guardian spirits at the beginning of the rainy season need not be understood as an "animistic substratum." Rather, it would appear to be a local ritualization of a canonical principle.

Canonical and post-canonical texts also include extensive discussions of magical power *(iddhi)*. Buddhas, *arahat* (those who have attained enlightenment), and *deva* are all thought to have miraculous powers including the ability to walk on water and through walls, fly, to have knowledge of previous births, the thoughts of others, etc. (Nyanamoli 1976: 409-446; Rhys Davids 1899, vol. 2: 88-89). Tambiah (1984: 45-49) has shown that this concept motivates much of the cult of *arahat* and amulets in modern Thailand.

While monks are forbidden to display magical powers, they played an essential role in the Buddha's enlightenment (Reynolds and Reynolds 1982: 12; Thomas 1975: 71-75). First he obtained knowledge of his own rebirths and then the ability to see those of others. It is the ability to "see" the *kamma* and past lives of others that enables the Buddha to teach the path to enlightenment to others.

While evil uses of power can be viewed as "non-Buddhist" when Buddhism is seen from the perspective of enlightenment, they are an integral component of Buddhist cosmological thought. Immediately before attaining enlightenment, the Buddha was confronted by the power of evil as personified in the demon Mara. Mara's army attempted to destroy the Buddha with magical weapons, thunderbolts, and other supernatural means, all of which were deflected by the power of the Buddha. Finally, he called the earth goddess to witness the merit he had acquired in previous lives, which gushed from her hair as a torrent of water, vanquishing the evil powers. Mara has power over all humans and tempts them to abandon the path leading to enlightenment. For our present purposes, it is significant that, like those who have attained enlightenment, he has enormous powers. What this implies is that power is amoral, even from the perspective of scriptural Buddhism. Rhys Davids (1899: 272-275) observed that, with the exception of *arahat* and the Buddha, magical powers are viewed as technical skills in exactly the same sense as carpentry and other trades. Even Devadata, the schismatic rebel who attempted to kill the Buddha, had great powers.

While the Theravada tradition clearly has a lay ethic, it remains ambiguous about the moral propriety of lay life. The purpose of lay Buddhism is to establish the conditions in which it is possible to trod the path to enlightenment. This aspiration means that the laity must support the members of the *sangha* who are directly involved in the quest for *nibbana* and perform meritorious deeds that will enable them to seek their own enlightenment in future lives. The ambiguity of lay life derives from the fact that it necessarily involves actions antithetical to these goals and perhaps more importantly because actions necessary to establish the religion may, at times, be, from a personal perspective, demeritorious. Similarly, the quest for merit may, in extreme cases, impinge upon the prosperity, and hence the ability to make merit, of others.

Discussions of kingship included in the textual tradition, particularly the *Jataka* stories concerning the former lives of the Buddha, provide cogent examples of this ambiguity. As Tambiah (1976: 39-53) has observed, the *cakkavatti* is the ideal king. He is a world conqueror whose realm extends to the lower reaches of the heavens. He is the lay counterpart of a Buddha. The Buddha teaches the *dhamma* (truth), and the *cakkavatti* rules in accord with it. He is the ideal king because he conquers, not with arms, but with the force of the truth. His rivals hurry to submit to him. Consequently, he avoids demeritorious acts, such as killing, that would normally be the consequence of conquest.

While the concept of the *cakkavatti* informs Buddhist kingship, the world monarch is an unrealizable ideal. The textual tradition also includes discussions of the moral and religious ambiguities of royal authority. In the *Vessantara Jataka* (Cowell 1957: 246-305), the future Buddha is a prince who is so intent on making merit through the practice of charity that he gives his wife, children, and a magical white elephant that ensures the prosperity of the kingdom to a wicked brahmin. The people of the kingdom are so outraged when he gives away the elephant that they demand he be banished. Because Prince Vessantara was the future Buddha, and because the story is a *Jataka*, it ends well. The elephant is recovered, Vessantara returns from exile, and the gods cause it to rain jewels so that he will always have enough to give away. The object of the text is to explain the perfection of charity and the merit derived from it. But, in another sense, it is an example of the tenuous balance between a king's duty to his subjects and his personal quest for merit. Southeast Asian kings, who could not depend on showers of jewels to support their deeds of merit, have not always fared so well. Generally, it is pagoda building, and not donations, which present problems. There is a well-known Burmese proverb stating, "The pagoda is finished and the country is ruined." The Burmese king Bodawpaya (reigning from 1782-1819), for example, spent years and vast sums attempting to complete what would have been the world's largest brick structure. The construction of this pagoda, which was abandoned when he died, very nearly bankrupted the state. One modern Burmese author (Aung Thaw 1972: 134) describes it as "the biggest brick pile in the world."

The association of kingship and demerit is the theme of the *Muga Pakkha Jataka* (Cowell 1957: 1-18). In this tale, the future Buddha is a prince who is so shocked by the demeritorious deed his father, the king, must perform, that he pretends to be mute. The text is very explicit about the dangers of kingship. The future Buddha's father is described as a just king. But when the prince is brought to the throne room, he sees his father passing judgement on criminals and remembers a series of former lives:

> I was king for twenty years and then I suffered eighty thousand years in the Ussada hell, and now again I am being born in this house of robbers, and my father, when four robbers were brought before him, uttered such cruel speech as must lead to hell; if I become a king, I shall be born again in hell and suffer great pain there. (Cowell 1957:3)

For present purposes, the conclusion to be drawn from these texts is that even the most exalted forms of lay life are morally ambiguous. They afford one the opportunity to make merit, but also necessarily entail demerit. Many Southeast Asian Buddhists are keenly aware of the ambiguity of their own lives. Burmese often explain that it is extremely difficult to adhere strictly to even one of the moral precepts. Only monks, whose conduct is governed by the *vinaya* moral codes, can avoid demerit.

To conclude, when Theravada Buddhism is seen as a totalistic religious tradition rather than a narrowly defined soteriological system, the Buddhological basis for the two religions theory falls away. Modes of action that do not, in any sense, contribute to the attainment of enlightenment are Buddhist to the extent that they are based on or interpreted in terms of Buddhist concepts. Indeed, the textual tradition recognizes the existence of evil beings and powers and the fact that lay life, even that of pious Buddhists, necessarily includes types of social action that conflict with the higher moral order leading to enlightenment. This does not, however, resolve the historical and ethnographic problems. If anything, it complicates them as it requires that the determination of the relationship between Theravada Buddhism as a universalistic tradition and local, non-Buddhist traditions be resolved on the basis of detailed, empirical investigation. The complexity of the textual tradition and the fact that it may motivate diverse modes of Buddhist piety (and in the case of evil, impiety) also motivates analysis of the material and cultural conditions that shape local social, ritual, economic, and political expressions of universalist principles.

The above issues are addressed in the papers by O'Connor and Tannenbaum. In a wide-reaching comparative study of Theravada Buddhist and animistic Thai societies, O'Connor examines relationships between trade, status, power, and modes of religious piety. The comparative study of Thai-speaking societies is an especially fertile field since it is the only extant case in which there are closely-related Theravada Buddhist (of several varieties) and animistic cultures. O'Connor argues that the conversion to Theravada Buddhism helped open Thai society to trade. Whereas earlier animistic religions focused on the 'fertility' of animals and crops, Buddhism set a precedent for accumulation and gift-giving. By grouping merchants together with other lay people in relation to the monastic order, Theravada Buddhism defined a legitimate social position for them. His contrast between Theravada Buddhist and 'tribal' Thai ritual is of particular interest. Pre-Buddhist Thai ritual defines boundaries and links local communities to particular spirits, while Buddhist rites define a center and leave peripheries open. O'Connor's view is that this practice is among the cultural factors that facilitated the development of lowland state systems.

The importance of giving in Theravada Buddhist ritual also fostered the development of trade and created a need for new types of goods. O'Connor observes that, from the perspective of a Theravada Buddhist state, this condition is paradoxical because to actively engage in trade diminished status. The probable cause for this state of affairs is that kings are required to be magnanimous to both monks and lay people. Consequently, kings were content to live from the profits of trade, but often disguised it as gifts or tribute.

Trade tended to languish under political systems of ascribed status, whereas it flourished in systems that emphasized status rivalry. While lower-scale merchant dealings might follow market principles, O'Connor clearly shows that in Thai Buddhist kingdoms, the elite's interest in trading varied according to the relationship between status and power in the polity.

O'Connor draws some of his comparative material on variant Buddhist traditions from the Shan, who speak a Tai language but occupy upland valleys in southern China, Assam, Thailand, and Burma. Their proximity to the uplands historically fostered close trading ties with hill peoples, and Shan was a lingua franca in much of northeastern Burma in the early 20th century. Prior to its abolition in 1885, many of the Shan states were political subordinates of the Burmese court in Mandalay. There are still close links between Shan and Burmese Buddhism. Since the early years of the 20th century, Shan have been among the major patrons of pagodas and other shrines in Mandalay. Moreover, large numbers of Shan, including some from Thailand, come to Mandalay to be ordained.

Tannenbaum's paper concerns relationships between upland concepts of power and Theravada Buddhism in Shan religion. She draws on Kirsch's (1973) model of upland power and potency, productivity, and ritual validation of status and argues that certain features of this cosmological view are also shared by the Shan. In a radical departure from former analyses, Tannenbaum argues that there are strong continuities in power concepts between upland peoples and lowland Shan that are related to the political and economic form of the latter's incorporation into a hierarchical Theravada Buddhist state. Cosmological power is not equally distributed throughout the universe, as all beings can be ranked in terms of their relative power. She argues that Shan peasants interpret many Buddhist practices through this idiom of power.

Although Shan share certain underlying axioms of power with upland groups, there are significant differences in how the Shan view gaining access to power. While power is morally neutral among both upland groups and the Shan, the latter gain power through the practice of Buddhist austerities and reliance on more powerful people. The Shan ideology of power is partly justified in terms of *kamma,* and people legitimize their claims to power through generosity and gift-giving to their dependents, monasteries, and monks. Monks are more powerful than the laity because they keep many more precepts. This ideology of power suggests that the textual theory of power is extended in Shan Buddhism to anyone keeping any number of precepts and is not restricted to those who have attained higher spiritual states.

Tannenbaum shows that keeping moral precepts is the basic component of Shan Buddhist piety and ritual. Precept-keeping among the Shan is a means of acquiring power that can be used for moral or evil purposes. Whereas O'Connor's paper illustrates the Siamese proclivity for joining merit and power, the Shan distinguish precept-linked power from merit.

Tannenbaum's exposition of the relationship between power and *kamma* raises important questions concerning relationships between morality, power, and Theravada Buddhist state systems. She argues that power exempts individuals from the consequences of their actions, at least in the short run. While Buddhologically-oriented scholars may question parts of her analysis, her argument is based on one of the very few recent ethnographic studies of Shan Buddhism. Overall, her paper suggests that the Shan variant of Theravada Buddhism differs significantly from the better-known Thai, Burmese, and Sri Lankan traditions and deserves more detailed attention.

While the Shan variant of Theravada Buddhism opens up a range of new questions for Thai and Burmese specialists, Shan relationships with upland societies in terms of trade, intermarriage, and political alliances have long been a major focus in debates on the causes of political variation and change among the Kachin. The lowland Shan and Thai are relatively stable hierarchical class societies, whereas upland societies are often characterized by oscillation between egalitarian and more hierarchical political forms. The next section briefly outlines the background of upland societies and the context of these debates.

Animistic Ritual, Power, and Economy

The mountain ranges extending southward from Tibet and China are populated by numerous ethnically and linguistically heterogeneous societies. With a few exceptions, upland economies are based on swidden cultivation and to varying degrees on trade. Political structure ranges from egalitarian village communities to hereditary chiefdoms. Most are animist, though many have converted to Christianity or Theravada Buddhism in the 19th and 20th centuries. Upland religious systems are characterized by concerns with agricultural fertility, magical power, ancestor cults, and formerly headhunting. As Lehman (personal communication) observes, this cult of fertility is most fully developed in areas of intense political and economic competition, such as the central Naga Hills, and to a lesser degree in the Chin Hills where conflict is not as pronounced. Hutton's summary of Naga religion would, with the exception of headhunting, apply equally to most of the upland societies of the region:

> the fertility of the crops and the prosperity of the village are closely associated with the dead, whose life-substance is conceived of as forming a continuous cycle of reproduction, passing from men to cereals sown, and thence back through grain eaten, or through the flesh of animals that have eaten it, to man again. It is this theory that forms the philosophic basis of headhunting, and while one of the forms of social status is acquired by the taking of heads and bringing additional life-substance to the community in that way, another is acquired by the distribution of acquired wealth and an attempt thus made by a successful man to inform his family, clan or fellow villagers with his superfluity of that life substance which is the secret of success. (Hutton 1921: 414-415)

Hutton's emphasis on power and fertility runs through most subsequent interpretations of upland religious traditions (Fürer-Haimendorf 1939, 1945, 1967; Leach 1954; Lehman 1963, 1977; Kirsch 1973). Friedman (1979) observes that in these societies economy and religion are so intertwined as to constitute a single system. Studies by Loeffler (1968) and Lehman (1977) indicate that kinship and marriage alliance are also included in this matrix. Relationships between sky, earth, and underworld closely resemble those between a lineage, its wife-givers, and its wife-takers in the asymmetric alliance systems common in the region. Power and potency pass from wife-giver to wife-taker and from sky to earth. Material wealth moves in the opposite direction, from wife-taker to wife-giver and from earth to sky and from the underworld to the earth.

Concepts of power and fertility may, therefore, be seen as among the principal cultural factors motivating social, political, and economic behavior. Ritual is employed to acquire power and fertility and to validate status. At the same time, ritual is among the primary means through which accumulated surplus is expended and redistributed. Fürer-Haimendorf describes these relationships as follows:

> The striving for social prestige on the part of the individual benefits the entire village community. For the need to accumulate large resources before a feast can be held, acts as an incentive to economic enterprise, and at the same time as a check on personal consumption. In the course of a feast of merit all the donor's accumulated resources are expended in the shape of sacrificial animals, whose meat is distributed, and of rice and beer used for the entertainment of the village. Thus the surplus wealth of prominent men is channelled to their fellow villagers and thereby transformed into merit and prestige accruing to the owner. (Fürer-Haimendorf 1967: 102)

Scholars are in general agreement concerning these features of upland religions, but they remain sharply divided concerning the causes of social and political variation in the region. Leach's (1954) classic study of the causes of Kachin oscillation between egalitarian and autocratic political forms focused on the role of external factors. Autocratic *(gumtsa)* political orders were modeled after those of the valley-dwelling Shan. The structural instability of Kachin political order was, however, ultimately produced by individuals manipulating cultural inconsistencies in their quest for power. Kirsch's (1973) essay focuses more explicitly on the internal religious cosmology and attributes political dynamism to individual desires to enhance ritual status and potency. Friedman (1979) emphasizes such ecological variables as soil fertility and population density, factors also noted by Leach (1954) and Kirsch (1973). Lehman (1977) and Maran (1967) have also focused on the role of trade and the complexities of ideological differences in Kachin politics. The final three papers in this volume provide a fresh look at these debates and the relationship between material and ideological causes of political oscillation.

Lehman's paper explores the effects of inflation on ritual, marriage alliance, and political systems of the Chin and Kachin of northern Burma. He demonstrates that while these systems are inherently inflationary, increased access to wealth resulting from contact with lowland societies may increase the level of inflation to such a degree that participation in the traditional status system is simply not worth the cost. Thus, inflation can bring on basic systemic change, foster the development of new modes of political authority, and, in extreme cases, bring about the abandonment of traditional religions in favor of Theravada Buddhism or Christianity. A salient theoretical point is that while material change can render a social/ritual system dysfunctional, it does not determine the course of future developments. Rather, it provokes cultural crisis and ethical debate concerning if and how a new system should be constituted.

Among the Chin, all types of status are, in principle, inherited. However, as inherited status must be validated by feasting, what is actually inherited is the right to compete for status. Aristocrats who fail to perform the required rituals become commoners, while commoners may be driven into slavery, becoming dependent on others for their status as social persona. Commoners may gain aristocratic status through strategic marriage alliances and feasts of merit.

The infusion of outside wealth allows upwardly mobile lineages to pay higher than normal bride prices that then become the "traditional" price. As other lineages raise their own prices, the cost of a "good" marriage may become prohibitive, leading to demands for either stabilization or abandonment of the system. The same is true of the feasting system, because aristocratic guests, who must validate the performance, demand higher and higher payments. Lehman points out that the result is a greatly decreased interest in feasting. Feasts cease to be a source of wealth and instead become, due to inflation, an economic liability. In other words, when ritual can no longer accomplish its stated goals, why bother to perform it?

Durrenberger's paper discusses feasting, economy, and the concept of power among the Lisu of northern Thailand. The Lisu differ from any of the Chin, Kachin, and Naga in that they are genuinely egalitarian. In this context, the entire notion of "feasts of merit" gives way to a ritual idiom based on curing. Durrenberger explains that a feast explicitly intended to establish hierarchical relations would fail because the potential audience would refuse to acknowledge it, or even to attend. Consequently, ceremonial exchange takes place in healing and other domestic rites. Obligations are horizontal between roughly equal households, rather than between superior and inferior households or lineages.

Durrenberger mentions that in the past there have been hierarchically organized Lisu. He combines Lehman's (1963, 1967) emphasis on the role of external trade with Kirsch's discussion of the ideology of potency and power in explaining political oscillation. He argues that opium cultivation and almost unrestricted access to lowland markets are the economic conditions fostering the development of egalitarian social formations among upland Southeast Asian peoples. Where wealth and access to market goods are scarce, hierarchic forms tend to arise. At least in the Lisu case, access to markets is a consequence of rapid lowland economic expansion and the associated extension of political control to hill areas in 20th century Thailand. All of the Lisu in northern Thailand are located within a few days walk of a Thai market town. Some villages are now "tourist attractions." It is not uncommon to see Lisu and other upland peoples on the streets of Chiang Mai purchasing supplies, eating in restaurants, and even playing video games. They have been integrated into national economic and political systems to a much greater degree than upland groups in other regions of mainland Southeast Asia.

Political and economic change have not, however, diminished the importance of the Lisu power/ritual/fertility complex. Power and fertility are derived from ceremonial feasting, though in an egalitarian context. Ancestors are still believed to be responsible for the well-being of their lineages. Relationships between the dead and the living, like those between households, are phrased in terms of mutual and approximately equal obligations rather than hierarchy. Thus, in a very different economic context, traditional religious concepts still inform social life and ritual performance but foster egalitarian rather than hierarchical social formations.

Woodward's paper concerns the Ao Naga of eastern Assam. Like other recent studies of the Naga (Friedman 1975, 1979), it is based on ethnographic materials collected in the early 19th century. The Ao are located between the plains of Assam and more remote Naga tribes in the interior. Their political system resembles that of the Haka Chin described by Lehman (in this volume). Status is acquired through feasting, which is open to men of any lineage. The feasting system is closely linked to trade because the principal sacrificial animal must be acquired from more remote tribes. The Ao cultivate some cash crops, which are sold in the plains, and act as middlemen in an extensive trade in ornaments, weapons, salt, and cattle with other tribes in the interior. Woodward presents a detailed account of the economic, political, and cosmological dimensions of the Ao mithan (Bos frontalis) sacrifice, which culminates a series of graded feasts of merit.

Woodward disputes Friedman's (1979) argument that upland egalitarian and autocratic social formations are largely ecologically determined. Whereas Friedman argues that Naga political systems are egalitarian because of ecological degradation and overpopulation, he counters that the Ao's seemingly egalitarian political structure is due to a cosmological system that does not allow any individual or social group to monopolize sources of magical potency. He also notes that Ao society was highly ranked in terms of feast sponsoring. Still, status enhancement only occurs in the context of rites that establish communal prosperity. The religious belief that feasting is the source of prosperity leads to the expenditure of resources on such a scale as to preclude the emergence of lasting class stratification. Moreover, the Ao, like the Lisu, are opposed in

16

principle to autocratic rule and may, again like the Lisu, kill those who seek to impose it.

Collectively, the papers in this volume make interesting contributions to our understanding of the highly variable relationships between ritual, power, and economy in the upland and lowland areas of mainland Southeast Asia. O'Connor argues that lowland political systems based on hereditary monopolization of power restrict trade. In the case of 'tribal' Thai and Lao Buddhists, authority rests on a ruling line's control of cosmological power. Lao royal ritual stresses the king's descent from gods, the veneration of images (linked to the king) and relics of the Buddha linked to pre-Buddhist fertility cults. Upland peoples and spirits were incorporated into the theory of kingship because they were the "original owners" of the land. The king must control these sources of power as well as those derived from Theravada Buddhist cosmological concepts. In contrast, Siamese (Central Thai) political systems are based on status. Royal legitimacy is based on merit acquired in previous lives. Status-based polities foster competition between and among elites, which in turn stimulates trade and an emphasis on gift-giving *(dana)* as a mode of Theravada Buddhist piety.

O'Connor places Shan Buddhism, which Tannenbaum shows emphasizes precept-keeping and the acquisition of power, between the achievement-oriented Siamese polity and the descent-oriented Lao kingdoms. Merit-making through donations to monks and temples among peasant Shan, in contrast to that of the elite in Buddhist kingdoms, may be either competitive or non-competitive since the ideological conception of a stable hierarchy of positions justifies even small offerings by poorer households.

Like O'Connor and Tannenbaum, Durrenberger emphasizes the role of cosmology in shaping economic behavior. Unlike O'Connor, however, he attributes more importance to the economic environment rather than to the form of status-oriented or achievement-oriented political forms. Competition for scarce goods will stimulate hierarchic, if unstable, political forms among the Lisu, whereas widespread access to wealth and goods fosters egalitarian forms. Lehman's analysis of Kachin and Chin emphasizes the conflicting principles of status and how they interact with not only spatial but historically changing economic conditions. His point that fluctuating access to new sources of wealth in upland systems underlies much of the political oscillation between egalitarian and hierarchical systems underscores the importance of examining ritual practice among different categories of the same population over time.

Lisu egalitarianism might be viewed as an extreme case of the inflation-driven social change Lehman describes for the Chin and Kachin. The economy, when compared to those of other upland groups, is so 'inflated' that the very basis of competition has been eliminated—if all

17

households have equal access to land and lowland resources, there are few resources to stimulate economic competition.

Like Lehman, Woodward emphasizes the ambiguities of ranking principles among Ao Naga, whose cosmology places restrictions on the intensity of status competition through feasting. In this regard, it is interesting to compare Ao beliefs concerning relationships between the feast-giver and the sky people with Lehman's account of the acquisition of aristocratic rank among Chin and Kachin. In both instances there is an element of hostility in the relationship that, when fueled by inflation, may in Lehman's terms "blow up" the system. Lehman shows that increasing the cost of status will lead some to opt out of the feasting system and that aristocrats are at least somewhat reluctant to validate the status of feast-givers. The Ao are concerned that the sky people will attempt to stop feasts of merit and will kill a man who gives too many feasts. Thus, what are political and economic disputes for the Chin and Kachin constitute religious dilemmas for the Ao.

It is our hope that these cases will stimulate further research into the parameters of continuity and variation between upland and lowland societies of mainland Southeast Asia. The specific way in which the issues raised here are analyzed, however, also represents a broader consensus among the authors as to how material and ideological processes underlie ritual practice and belief.

Ritual and Economy

While in general agreement with Sahlins (1976), Bourdieu (1977), Gudeman (1986), and others who maintain that the concept of economy cannot be considered apart from that of culturally defined systems of meaning, the authors in this volume are careful to consider both the effects of culture on material production and of the fluctuation of the availability of material resources and labor on social and religious action. From this perspective, social and ritual change may be seen as the product of either material or cultural phenomena. While rejecting any form of material or ecological determinism, they avoid the cultural determinism characteristic of much of what has come to be known as symbolic or interpretive anthropology.

The approach to ritual taken here is actor-centered and emphasizes the construction of representations of experience by individuals and the use of hierarchically organized knowledge systems in the production of cultural phenomena (including ritual) in social contexts. This approach does not grant ontological primacy to either ideas (or in the terminology of symbolic anthropology, 'meaning') or the "reality" of the material world. Individuals and societies do not respond to "natural forces" and ecological variables, but to conceptually interpreted representations of them. Material phenomena do not determine ideas, but may shape the ways in which they are socially articulated. Similarly, while ideas are not causes of material phenomena, they shape the ways in which humans respond to and seek to control their environments. Cultural change may, therefore, be driven by either material or ideational forces or by some combination of both. Lehman (in this volume) shows this very clearly in his discussion of the Chin and Kachin of northern Burma. Economic change, in this case inflation, may at times be responsible for the destruction of traditional ritual and political systems. It does not determine the constitution of "new orders," but rather sparks a political, ethical, and intellectual crisis to which there are several culturally plausible solutions. O'Connor's paper also points out that religious change, in this case conversion to Theravada Buddhism, altered the ways in which Thai peoples understood economy and, therefore, encouraged new types of economic behavior.

Ritual is understood as a mode of social and religious action that is necessarily public, but is, at the same time, rooted in the minds of participants and observers. A related notion is that the representational structures on which ritual is based presume the reality of "supernatural" beings, forces, and religious notions of causality. Ritual behavior is predicated upon metaphysical assumptions that, as Lehman (1972) and Keyes (1983) argue, need not be entirely conscious. Ritual is, from the perspective of the systems within which it is located, instrumental. Its purpose is to establish or transform relationships between human and other beings or to bend causal forces in a predetermined direction.

This theoretical perspective differs sharply from the symbolic or interpretive approach employed in most recent studies of ritual (compare Leach 1954; Geertz 1973, 1980, 1983; and Schieffelin 1985). Geertz (1983: 29-31) discusses what he sees as the two most common interpretive modes: the dramaturgical approach, understanding ritual (and other forms of social action) as cultural performance intended to reconcile differences or communicate meaning, and the social action as text approach derivative of Ricouer (1979), in which ritual is held to inscribe meaning.

As Shankman (1984) and Keesing (1982) have observed, interpretive methods have an unfortunate tendency to isolate cultural phenomena from their political and economic contexts as well as from the motives and beliefs of performers. While the analysis of cultural phenomena necessarily involves the use of concepts and conceptual schemata foreign to the tradition under analysis—such as the theoretical assumptions of the social sciences or humanities—current interpretive approaches often decontextualize ritual to such an extent that indigenous exegesis and the cosmological, social, and economic goals of ritual performance fade into obscurity. The problem here is not simply one of ethics, reflexivity, or accountability—"letting informants speak for themselves." It is fundamentally a question of explanatory and even descriptive adequacy, because indigenous understanding of what ritual intends to accomplish constitutes one of the central elements of any ritual tradition. Few, if any, of the participants in mainland Southeast Asian religious traditions would view their rituals as theatre or symbolic communication.

Ritual can be understood only if its goals and the methods it employs are taken as objects of analysis. Like Tambiah (1985: 123-166), the authors in this volume understand ritual as a set of constitutive acts. While it relies heavily on symbolic communication, the goals of ritual performance are cosmologically, socially, and in many cases economically defined. Symbolic communication is among the means through which ritual goals are accomplished. Dramaturgical performance, cosmological symbolism, and the expenditure of labor and material resources evoke meaning in the minds of participants and observers. As Sperber (1975) observes, meaning is constructed, not communicated. In the ritual context, performers act and speak in ways that, they hope, will result in the construction of a predetermined set of meanings in the minds of other participants and observers. Ritual succeeds only to the degree that an audience is convinced that its intended transformations are accomplished. This understanding is particularly important in rituals such as those described by Lehman, Durrenberger, and Woodward that alter the social standing of performers. What must be communicated is that the intended transformations have actually been accomplished and that the resultant status of the individual or group must be publicly recognized and acted upon.

A common problem with interpretive approaches to the study of ritual is, therefore, a confusion of ends and means. Symbolic communication is a vital component of ritual performance, but it is the message concerning the transformative power of ritual action and not the medium, which is of importance to participants. In this volume, Durrenberger makes this point very clearly when he writes, "The rituals do not really 'say' these things. Lisu are clever enough to think of less cumbersome ways to say things and parsimonious enough to think it foolish to expend such wealth on such a banal message." Ritual may be pragmatic, transcendental, or both. It is pragmatic action when the transformations it seeks to accomplish have bearing on, or are believed to affect the social, political power, fertility, prosperity, or well-being of individuals and social groups. Ritual is transcendental when these transformations are thought to foster the fulfillment of ultimate religious goals such as the attainment of enlightenment in the case of Theravada Buddhism or the journey of the soul to the land of the dead in the animistic societies of mainland Southeast Asia. Pragmatic and transcendental action are interdependent to the degree that the attainment of one set of goals requires the prior or simultaneous attainment of the other. Ritual performance is economic activity in that it requires the mobilization of labor and the expenditure of resources. As Bourdieu (1977) has argued, these expenditures are justified by the belief that ritual is among the sources of wealth, power, status, and position in the afterlife.

In these papers ritual is shown to be an appropriate arena for either cooperation or competition precisely because it draws upon the nonhuman sources of earthly well-being and prosperity. In mainland Southeast Asia, personal and communal well-being are understood to be a function of religious attainment. Consequently, the regulation of ritual activity may buttress hierarchical social formations when ritual performance is the prerogative of an elite, or buttress egalitarian systems when ritual competition is restricted.

Acknowledgments

We would like to thank Nancy Eberhardt (Knox College) for her critical comments and suggestions on an earlier draft of this introduction.

References

Aung Thaw
1972.   *Historical Sites in Burma.* Rangoon: Ministry of Union Culture, Government of Burma.

Boshe, J.
1971.   *Thailand: Land of the Free.* New York: Taplinger.

Bouquet, A.
1961.   *Comparative Religion.* London: Cassell.

Bourdieu, P.
1977.   *Outline of a Theory of Practice.* London: Cambridge University Press.

Cowell, E.
1957.   *The Jataka or Stories of the Buddha's Former Births.* Vol. 6. London: Luzac and Company.
Francis, H.
1957.   *The Jataka or Stories of the Buddha's Former Births.* Vol. 5. London: Luzac and Company.

Friedman, J.
1975.   "Economy as Religion and Religion as Economy." *Ethnos* 40 (1-4): 46-63.

1979.   *System Structure and Contradiction: The Evolution of Asiatic Social Formations.* Copenhagen: National Museum of Denmark.

Fürer-Haimendorf, C. von
1939.   *The Naked Naga*. London: Methuen.

1945.   "The Problem of Megalitic Cultures in Middle India." *Man in India* 25: 73-86.

1967.   *Morals and Merit*. Chicago: University of Chicago Press.

Geertz, C.
1973.   *The Interpretation of Cultures*. New York: Basic Books.

1980.   *Negara: The Theatre State in Nineteenth Century Bali*. Princeton: Princeton University Press.

1983.   *Local Knowledge*. New York: Basic Books.

Gudeman, S.
1986.   *Economics as Culture: Models and Metaphors of Livelihood*. London: Routledge and Kegan Paul.

Heine-Geldern, R.
1942.   "Conceptions of State and Kingship in Southeast Asia." *Far Eastern Quarterly* 2: 15-30.

Hutton, J.
1921.   *The Angami Naga*. London: Macmillan.

Keesing, R.
1982.   "Introduction." In *Rituals of Manhood: Male Initiation in Papua New Guinea*, edited by G. Herdt, 1-43. Berkeley: University of California Press.

Keyes, C.
1983.   "Introduction: The Study of Popular Ideas of Karma." In *Karma: An Anthropological Inquiry*, edited by C. Keyes and E. Daniels, 1-26. Berkeley: University of California Press.

1984.   "Mother or Mistress but Never a Monk." *American Ethnologist* 11: 223-241.

King, W.
1964.   *In Hope of Nibbana: The Ethics of Theravada Buddhism*. LaSalle: Open Court.

Kirsch, A. T.
1973.   *Feasting and Social Oscillation: Religion and Society in Upland Southeast Asia*. Cornell University Southeast Asia Program

Data Paper, no. 92. Ithaca: Southeast Asia Program, Cornell University.

Leach, E.
1954.   *Political Systems of Highland Burma.* London: Bell.

Ledi Sayadaw
1965.   *The Manuals of Buddhism.* Rangoon: Union Buddha Sasana Council.

Lehman, F. K.
1963.   *The Structure of Chin Society.* Urbana: University of Illinois Press.

1967.   "Ethnic Categories in Burma and the Theory of Social Systems." In *Southeast Asian Tribes, Minorities, and Nations,* vol. 1, edited by Peter Kunstadter, 93-124. Princeton: Princeton University Press.

1972.   "Doctrine, Practice and Belief in Theravada Buddhism." *Journal of Asian Studies* 31(2): 372-380.

1977.   "Kachin Social Categories and Methodological Sins." In *Language and Thought: Anthropological Issues,* edited by W. McCormick and S. Wurm, 229-249. The Hague: Mouton.

1987.   "Burmese Religion." In *Encyclopedia of Religion,* vol. 2, edited by M. Eliade. New York: Macmillan.

Lester, R.
1973.   *Theravada Buddhism in Southeast Asia.* Ann Arbor: University of Michigan Press.

Loeffler, L.
1968.   "Beast, Bird and Fish: An Essay in Southeast Asian Symbolism." In *Folk Religion and World View in the Southwestern Pacific,* 21-33. Tokyo: Keio Institute of Cultural and Linguistic Studies, Keio University.

Maran, LaRaw
1967.   "Towards a Basis for Understanding the Minorities of Burma: the Kachin Example." In *Southeast Asian Tribes, Minorities, and Nations,* vol. 1, edited by Peter Kunstadter, 125-146. Princeton: Princeton University Press.

Nyanamoli, Bhikkhu (translator)
1976.   *The Path of Purification (Visuddhimagga).* Berkeley: Shambala.

Reynolds, F.
1972.   "The Two Wheels of Dhamma: A Study of Early Buddhism."
          In *The Two Wheels of Dhamma: Essays on the Theravada
          Tradition in India and Ceylon,* edited by B. Smith, 6-30. AAR
          Studies in Religion, no. 3. Chambersburg: American Academy
          of Religion.

1978a.   "The Holy Emerald Jewel: Some Aspects of Buddhist
          Symbolism and Political Legitimation in Thailand and Laos."
          In *Religion and Legitimation of Power in Thailand, Laos and
          Burma,* edited by B. Smith, 175-193. Chambersburg: ANIMA.

1978b.   "Ritual and Social Hierarchy: An Aspect of Traditional Religion
          in Buddhist Laos." In *Religion and Legitimation of Power in
          Thailand, Laos and Burma,* edited by B. Smith, 166-174.
          Chambersburg: ANIMA.

Reynolds, F. and R. Clifford
1987.   "Theravada Buddhism." In *Encyclopedia of Religion,* vol. 14,
          edited by M. Eliade. New York: Macmillan.

Reynolds, F. and M. Reynolds
1982.   *Three Worlds According to King Ruang, A Thai Buddhist
          Cosmology.* Berkeley: Asian Humanities Press/Motilal
          Banarsidass.

Rhys Davids, T.
1890. (trans.)   *The Questions of King Malinda.* 2 vols. Oxford: Oxford
                 University Press.

1899. (trans.)   *Dialogues of the Buddha, Part 1. Sacred Books of the
                 Buddhists,* vol. 2. London: Luzac and Company.

1908.   *Early Buddhism.* London: A. Constable and Company.

1921. (trans.)   *Dialogues of the Buddha, Part 2.* Oxford: Oxford
                 University Press.

Ricouer, P.
1979.   "The Model of the Text: Meaningful Action Considered as
          Text." In *Interpretive Social Science: A Reader,* edited by Paul
          Rabinow and William Sullivan, 73-102. Berkeley: University of
          California Press.

Sahlins, M.
1976.   *Culture and Practical Reason.* Chicago: University of Chicago
          Press.

Schober, J.
1980.   "On Burmese Horoscopes." *Southeast Asian Review* 5: 43-56.

1984.   "Buddhist Pilgrimage in Burma." Paper presented at the meetings of the American Anthropological Association, Denver.

Schieffelin, E.
1985.   "Performance and the Cultural Construction of Reality." *American Ethnologist* 12: 707-724.

Shankman, P.
1984.   "The Thick and the Thin: On the Interpretive Program of Clifford Geertz." *Current Anthropology* 25(3): 261-279.

Smith, B. (editor)
1978.   *Religion and the Legitimation of Power in Thailand, Laos and Burma.* Chambersburg: ANIMA.

Sperber, D.
1975.   *Rethinking Symbolism.* Cambridge: Cambridge University Press.

Spiro, M.
1967.   *Burmese Supernaturalism.* Englewood Cliffs: Prentice Hall.

1970.   *Buddhism and Society: A Great Tradition and its Burmese Vissicitudes.* Berkeley: University of California Press.

Tambiah, S. J.
1970.   *Buddhism and Spirit Cults in North-east Thailand.* London: Cambridge University Press.

1976.   *World Conqueror and World Renouncer: A Study of Religion and Polity in Thailand against a Historical Background.* London: Cambridge University Press.

1977.   "The Galactic Polity: The Structure of Traditional Kingdoms in Southeast Asia." In *Anthropology and the Climate of Opinion,* edited by Stanley Freed, 69-97. New York: New York Academy of Sciences.

1984.   *The Buddhist Saints of the Forest and the Cult of Amulets.* Cambridge: Cambridge University Press.

1985 (1981). "A Performative Approach to Ritual." In *Culture, Thought, and Social Action,* 123-160. Cambridge: Harvard University Press.

Terwiel, B.
1979.   *Monks and Magic.* Copenhagen: Curzon Press.

Thomas, E.
1975.   *The Life of the Buddha as Legend and History.*   London: Routledge and Kegan Paul.

Weber, M.
1958.   *The Religion of India.* Glencoe: Free Press.

Woodward, F. (translator)
1933.   *The Book of Gradual Sayings.* Oxford: Oxford University Press.

CULTURAL NOTES ON TRADE AND THE TAI

Richard A. O'Connor

In the first millennium B.C., while trade, cities, and empires flourished, world-rejecting religions arose. In early India, Heitzman (1984: 131) sees a "threefold union of Buddhism, trade, and empire." Each grew with the others from roughly the 3rd century B.C. to the 3rd century A.D. Midway through this era, Southeast Asia began a similar synergy: as trade grew, Indic religions prospered, and chiefs became kings while villages turned into cities. Still later the Tai took a similar path. As they spread across Southeast Asia, each valley was its own realm ruled by lords little bigger than chiefs. Then Sukhothai (13th-15th centuries), rose to rule the others. It was or soon became Buddhist. Eventually it fell under yet another Tai Buddhist polity, Ayutthaya (14th-18th centuries), which fed on trade, finally giving the Tai the "threefold union"—Buddhism, trade, and empire—which had flourished in India over a millennium before.

What joined these three? Each needed or came to need the others, and so we must reject simple answers that split them apart to let one cause the others. Such lineal answers always put Buddhism last, legitimating merchants' wealth and rulers' power. That is naive. It makes the past serve the present's materialist faith that self-interest rules. So used, self-interest is an axiom, not an answer; and it is so broad it only tells us what we must first assume: people are rational. A deeper answer would explore how people constructed a world wherein they could act rationally. Here Buddhism did as much as trade and empire. Each had a hand in making past worlds where their partners were plausible.

We shall focus on early Tai trade (13th to 18th centuries), looking from first the polity and then the Buddhist point of a triangle. The remaining side, Buddhism and the polity, appears only in passing. It is crucial but well enough known (such as, Tambiah 1976 and Smith 1978) to ignore. Petty trade also appears only in passing, but for the opposite reason—we know too little—and because it came long before the threefold union. That leaves major trade by merchants, rulers, and rulers-cum-merchants. Where petty trade sought to get by in a subsistence economy, major trade amassed wealth in a prestige economy. In looking at major trade we must be thrice leery of the modern word "trade." It stresses exchange where the Tai elite wanted accumulation; it implies an occupation (that is, one's trade) where the Tai treated it as a tool; and, finally, for us trade is "on the market" and roughly within the law, whereas Tai trade mixed gifts and plunder. Following Weber (1947: 269), we might distinguish free from compulsory trade. The Tai knew both, although as the polity's power grew, so did the compulsory trade of tribute and monopolies.

Polity and Trade

That brings us to trade seen from the polity. From this angle, I shall not try to describe trade—who traded what with whom—so much as "place" trade within society. Where it fit conditioned what it was. To place it, we shall begin with the widest perspective, Tai culture, and work inward, following Tai distinctions. For clarity we must start with "free" trade as an ideal type.

Within Tai Culture: Trade versus Rule

Tai peoples have long known trade. In the earliest Tai writing, King Ramkamhaeng's inscription of 1292, Tai words *(kha-khai)* recognize trade as an activity distinct from, say, rule and religion. Since it stood apart, we can ask "where did trade 'fit' in society?" A clue lies in where this same inscription says the market was: outside the city *(muang)*. That put it, in one sense, "outside" of society.

To go beyond clues we must understand how society was organized. We shall use Condominas' (1980) view of Tai society as set up like Chinese boxes: the smallest "box," the family or household *(khrua* or *ruan)*, fit within the largest "box," the realm *(muang)* of a lord or *cao*. "Boxes" differed in scale, not form or function. From smallest to biggest, all were alike as social wholes, self-contained "families" ruled by one "father" or another. Everywhere this order Condominas calls emboxment was a, if not always the, principle of Tai social life. Whatever its manifestation, emboxment created an expansionist society that demanded attention to hierarchy (which "box" is bigger) and boundaries (inside vs. outside the "box"). We shall return to expansionism and hierarchy shortly, but for now the salience of boundaries helps us "place" trade and rule.

Boundaries: Boundaries set trade and rule apart. Trade was with the "outside"; rule was "inside." Whether the ruler was a father, village elder, or lord *(cao)*, his paternal benevolence earned the respect of his underlings likened to children or younger siblings.[1] While this patriarch could command their labor and crops, he also protected them and held rites for the commonweal. The "inside," whether as a household, village or realm, expected generosity.

"Free" trade clashed with these principles.[2] Practices that would have destroyed the "inside"—the give-and-take of barter, open self-interest, and specific and immediate exchange—posed no threat as long as trade was with the "outside." Of course that still left trade plenty of scope. After all, where "boxes" set within "boxes," what is seen as the outside depends on the box one is in. Trade, wrong within a household, might be all right within a village, was freer still between villages. Yet that did not make the larger realm a free market. Ruler and ruled could not trade openly without challenging familial solidarity. Trade went across boundaries, not within.

Trade's outwardness appears in its tendency to be or become ethnic. In the uplands the economic differences that made trade worthwhile often occurred between, and perhaps created, ethnic groups (see Peterson 1977). In the lowlands, from village to capital, ethnic minorities managed much of Ayutthaya's and Bangkok's trade (Smith 1980: 8-12; Ingram 1971: 19-20). If one follows Foster (1982), being "outsiders" protected traders from the generosity expected of "insiders." Then, too, it protected society from disintegration. It provided, as Geertz (1980: 38) says for Bali, an "ethnic insulation of the disruptive world of commerce...." Whatever the reason, trade's often ethnic character put it on the "outside."

Hierarchy: Along with boundaries, emboxment demanded attention to hierarchy: settling which "box" or leader was bigger than the others. Accordingly, Tai peoples often appear to be quite conscious of their place or status in society. While status was not always achieved, the structure of society and a bent for "big man" politics gave ambition great scope (O'Connor 1985a). To rise, a man had to attract followers, and that took wealth in land or goods. Trade was one way to get wealth to enhance one's status and perhaps solidify one's rule (O'Connor 1983; compare Wheatley 1983: ch. 5).

Status came from trade's riches, not trading itself.[3] Trading carried a stigma, at least for the Siamese elite. In the 17th century, la Loubère (1969: 83) reported that rulers of *muang* engaged in trade as if "they have some shame" in it, and two centuries later Low (1847: 398) noted that a ruler "is considered as lowering himself if he trades." Yet rulers needed trade, and so they put the taint on others. They delegated it to their underlings (la Loubère 1969: 83; Low 1847: 398), often non-Tai. Then too, their demand for gifts stripped trade of its vulgarity. Any trade with Ayutthaya's king was properly given as a "gift," even if it brought a "gift" of equal value in return (Wichitmatra 1973: 277-278, 311-312). Nor did this stop with the king. Late 17th century Dutch merchants found trade enmeshed in gifts. Each shipment demanded presents, and they had to make offerings for all sorts of ceremonies (Smith 1977: 96). Such customs and evasions let rulers be "mercantile without making them merchants..." (Geertz 1980: 96).

Why did rulers disdain trade? As burying trade in gifts reminds us, Tai lords were supposed to be magnanimous. Trade, on the other hand, could turn petty to make a profit. To be rulers they had to extol the "inside" and honor its values. Besides, as Indic rulers they presided over an intricate status hierarchy, and, as Weber (1958: 191) observes, in such systems "Very frequently every rational economic pursuit, and especially 'entrepreneurial activity,' is looked upon as a disqualification of status." Perhaps this is why other Indic rulers in Southeast Asia had similar attitudes (Geertz 1980: 38, 96; Hall 1985: 250; Trocki 1979: 53). In sum, a Tai ruler could find dignity in 'living off of' *(kin muang)* those he ruled (sometimes disposing of their surplus by trade) or foreign traders (taxing or extorting merchants), but he could not live honorably by trading.

Expansionism: Emboxment bred expansion. As Condominas (1980) shows, that is how the Tai spread so quickly across a huge expanse of Southeast Asia. They split off readily (such as sending princes off to found their own *muang* as each lord had his own household or "box"), made alliances easily (now on the "inside" as "brothers"), and, by war or marriage, incorporated ("emboxed") whatever groups stood in their way. Of course this did not end once the Tai ruled. Emboxment embodied what Durkheim (1964) called mechanical solidarity wherein the similarity (one "box" being like another) that held society together bred competition that made feuds, fissioning, and war endemic.

What did this imply for trade? Feuds, raids, and war hurt trade. They threatened not just the safety but the predictability trade needed to flourish. Nor could such a society, attuned to intrigue and daring, see any honor in trade.[4] For the upland Tai the right to bear arms with their lord set commoners above slaves (Condominas 1980: 289-294), thus linking status or honor to war. For the lowland Tai we know that every ruler and noble was also a military leader and that any man could rise or fall by his martial skills. Such a society could not extol trade, honor traders, or even insure the stability that might have let trade gradually take over.

Rule over Trade: While status-honor and martial virtues denigrated trade, rule and trade stood opposed as "inside" vs. "outside." Yet real opposition implies a worthy opponent, but here we see that trade always lost. And so, rather than depict them as two poles, rule vs. trade, we would do better to say rule subsumed "free" trade, turning most dealings into the compulsory trade of monopoly and obligatory "gifts." Rule's superiority was axiomatic and actual. It left traders as fair game, and, for rulers, it turned trade into just one means to amass wealth and thereby enhance their power.

Within Rule: Status versus Power

Whatever their prejudices, Tai rulers often tolerated or even sponsored trade. After all, rule required wealth. How much wealth? Obviously an upland Tai chief could thrive on a mere fraction of what Ayutthaya's opulent court needed to just "get by." That distinguishes between Tai polities by scale and complexity, but the trade-favoring need for wealth also varied within each polity according to its structure. Let me consider one dimension of this: a distinction between status and power. I shall argue that when status reigned it took more wealth to rule than when power was ascendant. As the status-power balance shifted, so did some conditions for trade.

By status I mean socially recognized honor or prestige, distinctions that culminated in the ruler and his court. By power I mean simple force that seizes what it wants, ignoring the subtleties and regularities status treasures. For the Tai, status and power properly and usually went together, but if separated they could become two poles defining a whole range of possibilities. Asserting power without proper status may have been vulgar or dangerous, but it was not unimaginable. Indeed, power was not an aberration but a culturally constituted possibility, perhaps born of status itself.

Our best example of this status-power duality comes from the Siamese Tai for whom Hanks (1962) first described these two poles as merit and power. Where people stood in society, their status, ultimately depended on their moral worth or merit (*bun*, karma), yet at any moment amoral power *(amnat, khaeng, khaeng-raeng)* could play a hand. Was one man's prosperity a consequence of his goodness, his merit, or an exercise of raw power? Only time would tell. Merit always triumphed in the long-run, but few knew how many moments or even lifetimes lay between then and now. So Hanks and the Siamese see as merit and power what I call status and power. We differ in that I use status to subsume merit. While that gets us away from Siamese life as they see it, a bit of distance helps us encompass earlier eras, other Tai, and even the region.

Can we generalize beyond the Siamese? I think so. In the region from India west to Polynesia many societies stress status and power in some mix. For Southeast Asia, Indianization created or perhaps just preserved this duality (O'Connor 1986a).[5] For the Tai this duality, itself implicit in the "inside"-"outside" distinction,[6] appears in Lao and Tai Yuan myths and royal rituals where autochthons possess a "power" that must be tapped by the more "civilized" Buddhist ruler, a person of high status and great merit.[7] While the consciousness and actual configuration of status and power seem to vary, the reality of a dualism does not.[8] Certainly all Tai stress status, and yet one need not look far to find power-shaping events— wars, raids, seizures, and assassinations abound—and then, if one looks long, power changes into status when the outcome endures.

What did this status-power complex imply for trade? Always mixed, status and power's implications appear once they are separated as ideal types. For power, trade was a resource like any other to seize or plunder. By itself power was too opportunistic and transitory to organize continuing major trade. When power came to the fore—unrest, plots, or war—one suspects regular trade fell by the wayside. For the ruler, its benefits came too slowly to alter an outcome; for the merchant, the risks grew. Status, on the other hand, was far more stable, and that in itself favored trade. While denigrating trade, status could still regularize it to the benefit of all. By allocating rights to organize and tax trade, status accepted trade within the polity.[9]

Of course I must reiterate that status and power only conditioned trade. They did not determine it. Remember that, as traders and consumers, other peoples had to want what Tai rulers were willing to sell or have sold. Our approach, looking through Tai culture, can say nothing about these outsiders, and its generality even slights the everyday Tai specifics that surrounded trade. Thus, status and power only make up the background, but then so long as power was a possibility, it constrained trade and kept it in its "place," beneath rule.

Within Status: Open versus Closed

Between the poles of status and power, trade had an affinity with status. Yet there was a more direct link between the two. Status, especially status rivalry, created a motive to trade and a market for prestige goods. This link rested on a cultural axiom: status was visible. Whatever its moral aura or spiritual essence, status manifested itself in the most material ways. In the *Traiphum*, a traditional Buddhist cosmography (see, for example, Reynolds 1976), the more merit a person had, the better looking, stronger, and richer he was (Lüthai 1982). Often the idiom was size. Rulers had bigger houses and held bigger ceremonies than the ruled. Indeed, one word for 'big' *(yai)* meant 'to rule' *(pen yai)* and another *(luang)* came to mean 'royal.' Buddhism accepted this. The bigger the gift, the more merit it made. In short, to be somebody in Tai society one needed some things—and the more the better. True, that in itself did not demand trade—many things came from within—but the better, more prestigious things often came from the outside.[10]

Yet if high status often demanded trade, how demanding was status? That varied. Ascribed status demanded less than achieved. In theory, trade varied accordingly, languishing under ascribed status and flourishing when achieved status goaded the elite to rivalry and demanded display. In practice, this condition seems roughly true, although sparse data, other variables, and the feedback between trade and achieved status preclude any clear test. And so, if only to illustrate this proposition, we shall consider a few cases.

Let me begin on the ascribed side with the Black Tai and White Tai. Their elite is hereditary, and rule itself is inherited. Rulers have a special link to the realm's supreme spirit. Only they can tap its beneficence so that the people can prosper. In sum, as history shows, their status is quite secure. It "fits," then, that for both peoples "commerce is not highly developed" (Lebar 1964: 221, 224; Dang 1972: 170; also see Silvestre 1918: 21, and Abadie 1924: 70 on the White Tai). Of course this is trade overall, not just the elite, but when rulers had to be wealthier than those they ruled, we must presume that they cannot have tolerated wealthy traders, at least among their Tai underlings.

32

Moving up in political scale, consider the difference between the Lü of Sipsong Phanna and the Burmese Shan. The Lü have a well entrenched hereditary elite. Succession to rule "is strictly patrilineal and by primogeniture" (Lebar 1964: 211). Only the ruling line can perform rites to the realm's supreme spirit. While Shan rulers are also hereditary, upward mobility is possible, and wealth is necessary to get or hold high status (Leach 1965: 214-215). Apparently rulers do not have a monopoly on sacrifice to the supreme spirit, and certainly Shan villagers in Thailand perform these rites freely (Tannenbaum n.d.). Being less secure in their status, we would expect the Shan elite to be more active in trade than the Lü, and that indeed appears to be true.[11]

Finally, for the largest and most complex polities, compare the Lao with the Siamese. In several ways, the Siamese stressed achieved status more than the Lao. For example, where Lao myths said rulers descended from the gods, the Siamese *Traiphum* gave everyone a human birth and made the king's superiority arise from his great moral deeds (Archaimbault 1959a, 1959b). Where Lao royal rituals recreated the genesis of the world and their kingdom, invoking both the past and descent, comparable Siamese rites displayed and thus established a hierarchy of achieved favor in an Indic present. Both Lao and Siamese ruled lands taken from earlier peoples, but where the Lao tried to rationalize their conquest in annual rituals, the Siamese left power to speak for itself. The Lao royalty of Lan Chang told how their founder had been sent from the Khmer court with a retinue, a great Buddha image, and a Khmer princess for his wife; in contrast, the Siamese rulers of Sukhothai told how they defeated the Khmer to win their independence. These and other examples (O'Connor 1985b) reveal a consistent set of Lao-Siamese distinctions—descent vs. ability, past vs. present, autochthon's or inheritor's vs. conqueror's rights—that put the Lao towards the ascribed and the Siamese towards the achieved pole of status.

Following our thesis, we would thus expect that the Siamese elite had a far greater stake in trade than their Lao brothers. Obviously that was true if we compare Ayutthaya to the Lao capitals of Luang Prabang and Vientiane, but—then what would one expect?—these upland Lao capitals simply did not have the trading opportunities that sea-linked Ayutthaya had. Of course, even if their locations did determine their difference, that would still not break the trade-achieved status link. It would just put trade first, creating a society open to achievement.

What about Sukhothai, the other Siamese capital? Its site did not favor trade, and so it is not surprising that like the Lao capitals it had only a fraction of Ayutthaya's commerce. Even so, apparently unlike Lao rulers, Sukhothai's King Ramkamhaeng openly declared that people could travel his realm without tolls and trade freely in several commodities, all without fear that he would confiscate their wealth. To modern eyes this practice appears to be a policy to promote trade, but it is far safer to say that the ruler simply accepted trade. In itself that is significant. After all, where status was rigidly ascribed, no ruler could have tolerated the disruptive effects of autonomous trade. While there is no direct evidence that Ramkamhaeng himself engaged in trade, his realm had many export-oriented kilns.[12] And so, by more modest standards and with far less certainty, we can say that just as Sukhothai emphasized achieved status more than the Lao, it favored trade more than its northern neighbors.

Before we move on to how Sukhothai and Ayutthaya differed, we need to consider their common dilemma. Earlier we noted that the structure of society, emboxment, let size settle ranking. For most Tai peoples, stability rested in making the biggest "box," the *muang*, hereditary in the ruling line. When the Siamese weakened this monopoly by "blood," size took on even greater weight. Where precedence once worked, now sheer eminence had to settle the ranking that held society together. That meant rulers had to have either great power or wealth, and either way it gave trade far more weight in deciding society's order.

Within Siamese Culture: Sukhothai versus Ayutthaya

Our steps inward finally bring us to the Siamese. Our last step went within status to link trade to achieved as opposed to ascribed status. This process lumped Sukhothai and Ayutthaya together because both stressed achieved status relatively more than the Lao. Yet here their status similarities end. Where early Sukhothai put status in an often simple Tai and Buddhist idiom with few ranks, Ayutthaya used an intricate Indic-Khmer idiom to institute an eventually elaborate social hierarchy. And so, unlike Sukhothai, Ayutthaya had to have trade to get the prestige goods its display of hierarchy demanded. Of course, if that tied Ayutthaya to trade, she can hardly have felt the bonds when she embraced trade anyway.

Why did Ayutthaya embrace trade? This question has many sides, from its founders' backgrounds to Chinese trade policy, but we shall focus on how the conditions of status competition set Ayutthaya apart from Sukhothai. As achieved status suggests, both polities stressed competition, but the locus of the contest differed. Sukhothai was engaged in a competition between elites scattered in its towns, whereas Ayutthaya was eventually absorbed in a competition within its elite. Where the first favored power, the second promoted status rivalry and thus trade. Let me consider each in turn.

Sukhothai: From perhaps the 7th to the 13th centuries the Tai spread across mainland Southeast Asia using alliance and conquest to establish their own polities. Sukhothai (13th to 15th centuries) arose in this era of power and initiated its end. It put many feuding Tai *muang* together into a larger polity where status began to supersede power. It did not, however, get very far. Consider early Sukhothai. In King Ramkamhaeng's inscription he calls his whole realm a *muang*, but then the lesser polities he rules are also *muang*. He has no special word to describe his realm as a *muang* above *muang*. Titles are roughly the same. He is a *khun*, apparently making him the leader of other lords, but this occurs in the compound 'father-lord' *(pho-khun)*, invoking a paternalism common to lesser rulers. Weaker still, he is a 'ruler of the *muang*' *(cao muang)* and king *(phraya)*, yet neither title is unique to his special standing; his underlings ruling their own *muang* could have claimed the same titles. In sum, his titles set Ramkamhaeng above ordinary men, but they did not recognize him as a king of kings. All of this tells us Sukhothai had yet to evolve the higher, center-defining status distinctions it needed to consolidate its authority as the preeminent *muang* among many. After all, if all the rulers were ranked clearly and absolutely, it would presume Sukhothai's many *muang* effectively had a single elite. Instead, the absence of overall ranking testifies to many elites scattered among many *muang*.

Ramkamhaeng's task was to subordinate these other elites and their *muang*. His policies seem designed to do just that—undermine internal rivals. Consider justice. He proclaims any commoner can come directly to him with any grievance (I/32-33).[13] What has happened to the commoner's immediate lord who, like any father, should handle such troubles? He has lost his patriarchal power. Indeed, what if the grievance was against that lord? Ramkamhaeng says, "When commoners or men or rank differ and disagree, [the king] examines the case to get at the truth and then settles it justly for them" (Inscription [I]/25-26 in Griswold and Prasert 1971: 207).[14] Or consider property and taxation. Anyone who clears new land and farms it or plants an orchard gets to keep it for himself and his heirs (I/23-24, II/5). He lets people trade freely and does not collect tolls (I/19-22). Did this undermine the privileges and revenues of petty lords? Surely some still ruled as their Khmer overlords had (and the word he uses for toll is from Old Khmer; Griswold and Prasert 1971: 206 fn. 21), while as Coedès (1954: 295) observes, Ramkamhaeng's policies show "a total opposition in all domains" to Khmer practices. Even his generosity challenges his rivals. He advertises it and invites others to prosper under him. If a ruler seeks his protection, he grants it; if that ruler has lost his wealth and subjects, he gives him some and helps him establish himself. While this may have added *muang* to his realm, it also undercut lesser rulers within his polity. After all, their disaffected lords, whether losers in succession disputes or those still waiting their chance, had a willing patron in the king.[15]

Unlike many later inscriptions and laws, Ramkamhaeng's prose is unpretentious, and he does not dwell on the niceties of status-defining rights and privileges and the allocation of honors and ownership. Of course we would expect this: status reigns within an elite, while we are suggesting a competition between elites, where power was more decisive. And so, instead of detailing status, we find the inscription praises power. It tells how Ramkamhaeng or "Rama the Bold" earned his name in battle; it extols his superiority "in bravery and courage, in strength and energy"; and it honors his ability "to subdue a throng of enemies" (Griswold and Prasert 1971: 204, 208). Such were the times. With many *muang*, each potentially autonomous and often ambitious, a leader had to be strong. History says as much. Again and again, later chronicles tell us this was an era of feuds between *muang*, each with its own elite.[16]

What does this imply for trade? Earlier we noted that struggles within an elite favor trade. Yet early Sukhothai shows a competition between elites where what you did or could do—your power—outweighed what you had to display. Of course its leaders did not have to reject trade to cultivate power, but they had to make some choices. Thus, apparently in pursuing power, Ramkamhaeng undermined his vassals by letting commoners trade freely and travel without tax. That surrendered the very rights that Ayutthaya's rulers used to conduct trade.

Ayutthaya: Sukhothai tried to rule a realm of many semi-autonomous *muang*, each with its own elite. Ayutthaya solved this problem by sending its own princes to rule four major surrounding *muang* (the *muang luk-luang*). That created a single elite. It took power (and marriage alliances) to pull off. Of course Sukhothai once had power, but unlike Ayutthaya it did not institutionalize the ritual distinctions of status that made a single elite (O'Connor 1983: ch. 6). Thus, where Sukhothai's ranking of lords and cities was often vague, Ayutthaya's seems to have been precise;[17] and where Sukhothai may have asserted Buddhist eminence, a claim others could challenge, Ayutthaya used Indic-Khmer distinctions that only the king could grant.

Apparently from the beginning, Ayutthaya took care to specify royal rights (such as Ramathibodi's claim to all the land; *Kotmai Tra Sam Duang* 1963: vol. 3, p. 115) that Sukhothai's rulers did not assert or even repudiated. If at Sukhothai this condition reflected efforts to undermine rival elites, Ayutthaya quickly established a single elite. Furthermore, where Sukhothai arose through power and found it a continuing concern, it seems reasonable to suppose that Ayutthaya's elite continued the status competition that probably had flourished under the Khmer at Lopburi.[18] Whatever the reason, Ayutthaya's king had the means to summon goods that he could use in trade. The first king probably had a warehouse to store taxes in kind and tribute, and at least by the mid-16th century King Chakkraphat claimed a monopoly in certain trade goods (Wichitmatra 1973: 111, 181). It is probably no accident that King Trailokanat (1448-1483), whose laws were the first to specify (or reclaim?) tolls, was also the king under whom the court "entered consciously into foreign trade" (Viraphol 1977: 19).

Once established, having a single elite changed politics. Charnvit (1976: 104) describes this as a shift from petty *muang* politics, where each struggled for independence, to a competition for influence at the center,

Ayutthaya. Put in our terms, a struggle between elites that favored power changed into competition within an elite that favored status and thus, indirectly, trade.

Yet not everyone could trade, nor could Ayutthaya live by trade alone. Like earlier Tai *muang*, it also had to control manpower to field an army, farm the land, build temples, or stage ceremonies. Where some in the elite managed trade, others controlled manpower. The split was not accidental. Kings practiced divide and rule, but that the division should end up more or less as "trade vs. manpower" testifies first to trade's tension with status-honor and finally to the inherent possibilities of each sort of resource.

While the center "owned" everything symbolically, in practice, trade outdid manpower as a way to realize its claims. One could centralize trade physically by controlling foreigners and drawing goods to the capital or royal ports, but one could not keep manpower in the center for long. Yes, one could summon them to fight a war or build a temple, but most of the time manpower had to be dispersed to fill and farm the country. Moreover, as the realm grew larger, travel time increased, and it became more and more inefficient to draw manpower into the center. Tribute that one could turn into trade was worth more than corvée one could not summon. Furthermore, one could store and accumulate trade goods, but manpower had to be used or lost. Administratively it was the same story, although for traditional rather than rational reasons. Trade was built on taxes sanctioned by Buddhism (10 percent for the king) and the ancient practice of offering part to the ruler who then made offerings to the gods. Royal monopolies on particular goods also had symbolic and perhaps historical affinities with taboos that reserved some things for the gods. Finally, as trade was outside of everyday household life, the king could properly claim it as he claimed all unowned land and goods; and as trade was potentially disruptive (its tension with status) and sometimes dishonest, he had a duty to regulate it the way he kept crime and unrest in check.[19] In contrast, tradition went against the king asserting such complete control of manpower. It violated the status of his underlings. When society was so many households within households (that is, "boxes" within "boxes"), he had to honor the perquisites of household heads from princes to peasants, each of whom had to have his own dependents. In fact, every person of position had a specific right to a certain number of dependents, and the king could never claim even the slave of a peasant.[20]

Like other Tai polities, Ayutthaya grew by drawing, literally or symbolically, more and more of life into the center and its status hierarchy. Given their intrinsic and traditional differences, that made trade a more effective agent of centralization than manpower. And so, trade in the abstract an enemy of status-honor, became in practice its functional ally. Yet this trade-status nexus faced a danger. As it grew more intricate, more centralized, it lost control of the inevitably dispersed manpower. Where the trading elite benefited from the stability and elaboration of status, the manpower elite could counter with the Tai alternative—power. When these lords could not win in the trade-inflated status competition, they had only to arm their followers to seize a palace, sit out a war, or side with an enemy.

Ayutthaya's history testifies to the center's recurrent failure to keep the loyalty of its manpower and their leaders. When in 1569 a large Burmese army attacked Ayutthaya, the capital proved unable to summon its manpower (Wyatt 1984: 97-98) and soon fell to the invaders. The Burmese installed as vassal one of the Tai provincial lords who had first resisted Ayutthaya's control and then finally added his manpower to the attacking Burmese.

In the next reign, King Naresuan (1590-1605) restructured the Siamese polity. Early Ayutthaya had sent its princes out to rule key *muang*, subordinating their elites to Ayutthaya's ruling line. As long as these other elites were serious rivals, their threat ensured the loyalty of these princes. Once that threat was gone, these princes posed a threat to Ayutthaya. They had royal blood and controlled manpower. Naresuan's solution was to bring the princes into the capital where they were away from their manpower and more easily controlled by the king. In effect, this was a further ritual distinction of status that put the capital still higher above the provinces now ruled by non-royal officials. Once again, the power struggle between *muang* had been brought into the capital where it could be turned into status competition. It fits our theory, then, that the following reign saw "a dramatic expansion of foreign trade" (Wyatt 1984: 107), and that by the mid-17th century from a quarter to a third of state income came from royal monopolies that often served trade (Viraphol 1977: 19).

Yet Naresuan's reorganization cannot have ended the intrinsic differences between control of trade and manpower. Therefore, the center's eager absorption in trade and status competition was periodically rocked by power as "virtually all successions...in the seventeenth and eighteenth centuries were, at the least, irregular, and, in many cases...usurpations" (Wyatt 1984: 105). In line with this, Ayutthaya continued to have difficulty controlling manpower, and when the Burmese attacked in 1767, once again the capital fell when it could not summon enough manpower (Wyatt 1984: 108, 137).

Buddhism

Now we turn to the other side of our triangle: trade and Buddhism. So far, looking at trade from the polity, our steps inward have tried to place trade within Tai and especially Siamese culture. Where we found change, it was often an oscillation, a movement between poles. Now we need to consider a deeper change: Buddhism. By altering the configuration of Tai culture, Buddhism changed "where" trade fit within society and "why" society took to trade. We shall use the symbolic implications of Buddhism and its actual Tai varieties to tease out the transformation of society Kirsch (1977) calls Buddhaization.

Within Religion

Buddhaization: To understand how Buddhism changed the Tai we must consider their earlier religion. Often called animism, a name that reflects its principle, we shall be more concerned with its objective: "fertility"—getting rain and health, making crops and children grow. This was not unique to the Tai. Hocart (1970) argues that all early religion promoted "life," and Boon (1983) shows how this concern set up a tension of extremes. For the Tai, these extremes can be put as oppositions: male vs. female, sky vs. earth, up vs. down, outer vs. inner, and so on. A complete list is neither necessary nor possible. Here, what matters is that ritual joined opposites to strengthen or even create "life." These were not esoteric rites. They were as obvious as procreation. Indeed, some upland Tai rites of spring that joined male and female symbols, also let men and women join during a period of sexual license (Bonifacy 1915; Maspero 1950: 153-154).

As Boon (1983: 214-216) has shown, Buddhism presumed a radically different order. Monasticism not only stood outside of society, its celibacy denied the literal and symbolic "life-giving" union of male and female. Instead of male-female, Buddhism offered monk-lay relations. Yet this set up a hierarchy on a single principle (the superiority of asceticism), not a balance of opposites. In a word, Buddhism was monistic, not dualistic. Moreover, as a reformist creed, it could not just posit one ultimate reality, it had to devalue "life-giving" oppositions as the root of suffering and pitfalls in its quest for what Hocart (1970: ch. 6) called the "good"—moral growth and ethical progress.

Of course Buddhism's higher goals left room for earlier wants. Today, the old religion lives on alongside or within the new. Fertility rituals make monks one pole in their ancient opposition, or even fit Buddha relics and images to opposing poles (O'Connor 1985b). Yet amid this common syncretism, Tai do differ in how much Buddhism eroded "life." Consider myths of the Rice Mother, fertility herself, and the Buddha. In one Shan tale the Rice Mother beats the Buddha in a contest to see who is more powerful (Durrenburger 1980: 48-50). He fares better in the Lao myth Tambiah (1970: 351-361) reports for a northeastern Thai village. The tale not only incorporates "ethical statements," it says that "rice came along with religion" [Buddhism], "to feed life and religion." Finally, the Siamese know the Rice Mother well (J. Hanks 1960), but Textor (1973: 821) says in Bang Chan she lacks the elaborate mythology Tambiah reports.[21] And so, the Rice Mother goes from superiority, through complementarity, to the inferiority of being just one among many deities, all beneath the Buddha.

Each step marks further Buddhaization that puts "life" in its place as a real but lesser concern.

Lao "Fertility" vs. Siamese "Order": Let me now focus on Buddhaization where it concerns us most: the top of complex polities. Here the Lao come closest to the Siamese, and so their differences take on greater weight. To state the contrast sharply, where the Lao stressed the "fertility" of the old religion, the Siamese doted on "order" implied by the new.

Each Lao polity (*muang*) had its own rituals, but all sought "life"— the protection, renewal and rain we shall call simply "fertility." They sacrificed buffalo "to change the seasons, desacralize the soil and predict, if not control, rain" (Archaimbault 1975: 131). They worshipped at Buddhist stupas (*that*) which, as Mus (1975) has shown, built upon autochthonous fertility cults. While stupas held relics linked to the land, great Buddha images were linked to the king (O'Connor 1985b). With both relics and images as palladia, their Buddhism conformed to the earlier religion's dualism. Annual rituals re-enacted the creation of the human world, recreated the kingdom, and legitimized the Lao and their ruler's possession of the land they had seized from earlier peoples (Archaimbault 1964, 1973). Although conquered, these tribal peoples still had "power": they held "the key to the control of local spirits" (Chamberlain 1986: 63), the very beings whose blessings made the fields fertile. To tap this native and chthonic power, it was represented as one pole that ritual joined to the Lao and the sky on the other pole. Therefore, opposition was vital, indeed vitalizing. In key royal rituals, as Archaimbault (1964: 1973) has shown, the king or his men were one pole; the other was, variously, autochthonous peoples, commoners, or "rebels"; and their opposition crystallized in boat racing and hockey (*ti-khi*) contests. Incorporating competition recognized contrary principles, such as distinguishing male from female, which allowed their fruitful union.

In contrast, in the Siamese polity's rituals fertility was not their object nor opposition their principle. Buffalo sacrifice either declined or was never vital.[22] The stupa or relic cult also declined as images won favor (O'Connor 1985b), thus putting the royal and conqueror's side above the autochthonous one. Indeed, major state rituals drop autochthonous peoples, and thus the chance to tap their fructifying powers. While both Siamese and Lao had New Year fertility rites (*songkran*)—where images, monks, and elders were sprinkled with water—la Loubère (1969: 117) says the Lao ceremony differed in that "the king himself is washed in the River." Presumably la Loubère's Siamese informants saw this as a significant difference; certainly that difference implied some reserve towards fertility rites and kept the ruler above being just one of two poles. In the late 17th century one king gave up the ritual to make the waters recede for harvest, and long before that kings had delegated the first plowing ritual to an underling (la Loubère 1969: 20, 43). To delegate this fertility rite put the king above its oppositions, suggesting he embodied a single principle rather than one of two contrary ones. That left fertility a lesser concern and gave it a lower status, but then what would one expect from a court absorbed in trade, war, and display? Surely peasants worried more about fertility than their often distant rulers.

What worried the Siamese elite? Ranking. Major royal rituals ranked everyone at court, and, judging by 19th century archival documents, these rites had many nuances to express royal favor. Lesser rituals held by nobles showed whom they favored, displayed their wealth, and documented their social position. True, Lao rituals also displayed rank, but with a simpler hierarchy and positions more readily secured by descent the Lao had little of the ambiguity that drove the Siamese elite to establish where they stood. It is also true that Siamese rituals sought fertility, but can this have been much more than convention, a legacy of ancient rites now turned to other ends? If fertility was vestigial and ranking key, then it appears that these rites legitimated the elite not to the peasants but to each other.[23] Hints of this appear in Siamese festivals and ritual competitions. According to Barros in the 16th century, officials were "required periodically to show their skill in arms at festivals" in Ayutthaya (Lach 1965: 530), clearly a competition within the elite. Similarly, Archaimbault (1973: 73 fn. 15) notes that the ritual game where the Lao pitted representatives of the king against autochthonous peoples was played at Ayutthaya between the capital and provincial courts. Thus, the opposition that the Lao invoked in fertility rites the Siamese used to embody struggles within the elite.

Siamese rituals that ranked people cannot have readily upheld the tension of opposites fertility demanded. After all, ranking went by a single principle. Unlike fertility, whose dualism appeared again and again from capital to household, Siamese ranking was unitary and absolute, its peak fixed in the king. Such an order could not and did not recognize an opposing power as the Lao did with autochthons. Besides, it did not need to. To rank people created "order" in society; with order Buddhism prospered; and that took care of fertility. This last step is what Reynolds (1985: 77) identifies as "the traditional belief that Dhammic activity in the religio-moral realm will assure the proper functioning of nature."

By downplaying dualism and putting fertility under "order," the Siamese took Buddhaization further than the Lao. Like merit or karma, society ranked all people. Indeed, social and moral hierarchies were equated. Now, if all Buddhist peoples moved towards this equation, to move far they had to subordinate more and more of life to a single principle. Here the Siamese went further than other Tai. Instead of a dualism that joined opposites to unleash a "life"-promoting power, Siamese rituals moved towards a sober monism whose simple consistency promised "good."

41

Buddhism and Trade: What did this imply for trade? Buddhism, a religion to end craving, could create new needs. To understand how, consider what Hocart (1970: 72) says. Where early religions settled for material prosperity, ethical religions such as Buddhism wanted that and something more: goodness. So it was not enough to bring the rains and banish disease; one also had to do good or, as Buddhists say, make merit. Merit-making knew no practical limit—was there ever enough good in a world of pain and suffering? Unlike earlier religions that were satisfied once the rains came or the plague left, with Buddhism one did not know where to stop. Indeed, how could one stop when the goal was not present pleasure but future birth? In sum, where earlier religion's specific goals fit a world of specific needs, Buddhism's almost endless quest opened up the possibility of enormous needs. That quest did not make the devout into traders, but it did make trade plausible in a new way.

If religious ends seem too abstract, consider their means: dualism's efficacy came from the union of opposites, while monism tapped asceticism through gifts. True, both religions saw a large offering as better than a small one, but dualism's first demand was a correct ritual. Therefore, a Tai who could not afford a buffalo, sacrificed a chicken; and if a chicken was too dear, an egg would do; but any offering correctly done might work to bring the rain or cure your kin. One could even haggle with a spirit—if a small offering failed, you tried a bigger one. In contrast, Buddhism did not accept bargaining. Giving to a proper monk, one got exactly what one gave. In effect, eroding dualism left size as the ruling principle, and so balance gave way to bigness.

Let me put this in Siamese context. We can see Buddhism's affinity with greater needs if we contrast it with animism. Earlier we noted that a sacrifice had to be correct, not necessarily extravagant, and that is quite close to what Ramkamhaeng says about offerings to the supreme spirit of his *muang*: if the king "makes obeisance to him properly, with the right offerings, this kingdom will endure...but if obeisance is not made properly or the offerings are not right,...the kingdom will be lost" (Griswold and Prasert 1971: 214). If the offerings were extravagant, he does not say they were, and so evidently their size did not matter much. Contrast this with how he records offerings for a Buddhist *kathin* ceremony: "heaps of cowries,...heaps of areca nuts,...heaps of flowers, with cushions and pillows: the gifts...[amount to] two million each year" (Griswold and Prasert 1971: 209). Here the size of the offerings matter. It also virtually invites competition: can your *muang* better this? Like making merit, such competition knew no end. Buddhism, therefore, created new needs.

Within Buddhism

Of course Buddhism varied. If all Buddhists had new needs, Tai peoples differed in the kind and intensity of their wants. As Keyes (1983:

42

267) says, merit-making may have been "equated with religious action," but they knew there were other paths: "*panna*, 'wisdom,' and *samadhi*, 'mental discipline,' as well as *sila*, 'morality'..." Where merit-making often ended up as gift-giving, these less favored paths followed ethics (Tambiah 1970: 148), meditation, and asceticism. Mixing these possibilities let each Tai people fashion their own Buddhist tradition.

Siamese vs. Other Tai Buddhists: To get some sense of the Siamese style of Buddhism, we can contrast it to other Tai Buddhist traditions. Consider Shan and Tai Yuan. Both stress the lay asceticism of following precepts much more than the Siamese.[24] Where they readily rank people by the number of precepts they follow (Kingshill 1960: 141; Tannenbaum n.d.), the Siamese would be quick to factor in one's merit-making gifts and slow to let precepts overturn ranking by titles and positions.[25] And so, it is appropriate and, as Kingshill (1960: 98) suggests, "perhaps ... significant" that Shan and Tai Yuan call the Buddhist holy day 'precept day' *(wan sin)*. By the same token, the Siamese word *(wan phra)*, 'the lord's (or monks') day,' invokes a hierarchical and categorical distinction (Buddha/monks vs. laity) rather than the relative difference in precepts.[26]

Even within gift-giving the Tai differ. The Tai Yuan have a tradition of texts, *anisong*, that specify the merit to be made by a particular deed (Keyes 1983: 275-276; Davis 1984). That difference robs gift-giving of the competitive edge it has for the Siamese. After all, equating all gifts of a similar kind undermines invidious distinctions arising from the actual cost of the ceremony. One modern *anisong* even says that, lavish or poor, an ordination makes the same merit for its sponsor (Thammachak 1971: 69-70). Tai Lü villagers go still further: they sponsor ordinations collectively, rejecting the Siamese practice of letting one person or family get all the merit and honor of the gift (Moerman 1966: 150).

Moving from village to court, Luang Prabang's and Ayutthaya's ceremonies reflect the differences between Lao and Siamese Buddhist traditions. While both polities had ceremonies for every month, Reynolds (1978) argues that Luang Prabang stressed three festivals: a calendric New Year (November) when the king lustrated monks; a traditional New Year (*songkran* in March-April) focused on a Buddha image (the *phrabang*); and a stupa festival (October) centered on the realm's great Buddha relic. All three rites renewed the realm and brought prosperity. For Ayutthaya, la Loubère (1969: 43) says the king appeared in public only twice a year when he made offerings to the monks. This pattern fits the testimony of Ayutthaya's survivors (Damrong 1967: 265-270). While they mention ceremonies for every month, there appear to be only two major annual Buddhist rituals: the traditional New Year and the *kathin*, an offering made at the end of lent.[27]

Comparing Lao and Siamese, we see one ceremony in common: the traditional New Year where both honored the image that was the realm's palladium. We also see a key difference: the Siamese did not emphasize a relic festival. All of this fits our earlier distinction between fertility and "order." Where the Lao stressed the two poles, image and relic, the more monistic Siamese emphasized just the image, itself associated with kings, and neglected the relic linked to autochthonous peoples and ancient fertility cults. Yet this is only part of their difference. Note what festival the Siamese stressed and the Lao did not: the *kathin*, a gift-giving ceremony. Note, too, that this ceremony was done for all to see, and that the king's only other public appearance was also to present gifts to monks (la Loubère 1969: 43). This was not just Ayutthaya. If we go back in time to another Siamese people, we find that Ramkamhaeng's inscription treats the *kathin* as Sukhothai's preeminent ritual. If we go forward to Bangkok, it is clear that royal *kathin* displayed wealth as well as rank and royal favor. They not only demanded great gifts, they asserted the king's ownership of the realm's major temples.[28]

Why did the Siamese put such stress on gift-giving? Surely trade did more than pay for the elite's extravagant gifts. Anything so central to Ayutthaya's court almost had to shape their style of religion. Yet what about Sukhothai? It also stressed gifts, but these must have come from tribute and booty more than trade. Perhaps it is better, therefore, to say wealth, not just trade, shaped religion. That is a start anyway, but to link wealth to religious style we need to answer two questions: First, why display wealth? Second, among many possible displays, why did they favor Buddhist gift-giving?

Why Display Wealth?: While rule required wealth, wealth did not require display. One could bury gold or use it for bribes. Ingratiating superiors or helping followers could be costly without being public. Given other possibilities, why did display take on such salience that it may have shaped religion? Display flourished when status rivalry raged, and such competition arose from society's structure, its center-defining status distinctions. Earlier we discussed how this structure conditioned status and power; now we shall consider how it shaped religion.

Let me state this as a principle: the more intense status competition was, the more it favored a relative shift (it cannot have been absolute as the two were interdependent) from asceticism to gift-giving as the way to make merit. Why? Buddhist symbols gave the Tai only certain possibilities. Asceticism did not lend itself to competition.[29] Extreme austerities violated the Buddha's advice to follow the Middle Way. Besides, anyone rich or poor could undertake asceticism, and that undermined the status hierarchy that competition aimed to set. In contrast, gift-giving was easily turned to competition. How much one gave came to measure one's social standing. As competition inflated the gifts, only the wealthiest could claim high standing.

Does this "principle" given by the symbols fit the events given by the past? Let us compare two descriptions of Sukhothai *kathin*, one by Ramkamhaeng and the other by his grandson Lüthai nearly seventy years later (Griswold and Prasert 1971; 1973, Inscriptions 4 and 5). By the later ceremony, the gift has increased several fold and lay asceticism has lost prominence.[30] Where Ramkamhaeng says that all of the elite observed the precepts during lent, Lüthai says nothing. Either they did nothing or for him, unlike his grandfather, what they did was not worth mentioning. Elsewhere in his inscription Ramkamhaeng says, "The people like to observe the precepts..." and refers to "the throng of lay people who observe the precepts" on Buddhist holy days (Griswold and Prasert 1971: 209, 214). In contrast, Lüthai's inscriptions are silent on lay asceticism.[31]

We would expect these two changes if status competition had increased. Had it? Yes, judging by the *kathin*. As Ramkamhaeng describes it, the elite or perhaps the whole populace made the offering (I/8-14). He could have said he made it (for example, at II/28-29 he does say he built a monastery), but he does not. A collective gift left no room for status competition, not within the elite anyway. In contrast, his grandson Lüthai says that the major *kathin* offering is his gift, and he distinguishes this from "the accessory [offerings] brought by members of the royal family and nobility..." (Inscription 5, III/19-20, Griswold and Prasert 1973: 158-159). What counts now is not what all gave together, but who gave how much. As the king distinguishes his gift from what the royalty and nobility gave, can they have not distinguished between their gifts; and as the king specifies how much he gave, can they have ignored what each of them gave? All of this testifies to greater status competition within the elite.

Why had such rivalry increased? We can get some clues by continuing our comparison of Ramkamhaeng's and Lüthai's polities. Earlier we said that Ramkamhaeng's realm had many *muang*, each with its own elite, and that the consequent competition between elites favored an emphasis on power over status. Lüthai faced much the same problem. In fact, sometime after Ramkamhaeng, many *muang* had split away to become independent and only Lüthai's power had forced them back into the realm. Obviously his grandfather had failed to consolidate the realm. He had not turned these many elites into a single elite, and so this was now Lüthai's task. This had two sides: undermining the old elites and creating a new one. His policies (Inscription 3, II/23-47, Griswold and Prasert 1973) echoed Ramkamhaeng's, and like them would indeed have undermined lesser lords. He also vigorously promoted Buddhism, even building shrines in *muang* ruled by lesser lords (Nagara Jum and Sralvan). This activity worked two ways. It undermined old elites, either non-Buddhist Tai lords or erstwhile vassals of the Khmer still tied to earlier symbols; at the same time, it provided the symbols to construct a new elite.[32]

If Lüthai had succeeded in creating the rudiments of a new elite, this shift might explain the increase in status competition—perhaps a single Buddhist idiom was turning the old power struggle between elites into competitive gift-giving within an emerging elite. Yet there is another, simpler explanation: factions within Sukhothai's own elite. We have no evidence of factions in Ramkamhaeng's day, but perhaps soon after his reign Inscription 2 hints at a split. As Gosling (1983: 299-301, 307) observes, its author, apparently a monk, claims a descent from legendary Tai heroes that differs from and perhaps betters the rulers' ancestry. Other events in that era also suggest a struggle between the ruler and the Sangha as well as between the sister cities, Sukhothai and Si Satchanalai (Gosling 1983: 299-301, 307; O'Connor 1985b). Lüthai's reign began by his seizing Sukhothai from a usurper (was it someone from the rival line?), and if these rivals remained within his court, then this, too, could explain the status competition. Whatever its origin, its implications are clear: rivalry favored display that shaped the Siamese style of Buddhism.

Turning to Ayutthaya, we also find display. We would expect that. Its success as a polity, institutionalizing the center-defining status distinctions discussed earlier, made the capital into an arena for rivalry. Sumptuary laws restricted many displays, but there were a few ways to show one's wealth. For example, la Loubère (1969: 27) notes that on the last three fingers of each hand they wore as many rings "as possibly can be kept on" and that the young of "good Family" wore bracelets on arms and legs.

But these displays were trivial beside the gifts that flowed to Buddhism. People of moderate means gave images to temples (la Loubère 1969: 124), but the highest gift was to build a temple, a very costly offering. Yet, perhaps driven by rivalry, the expense did not deter the wealthy. To quote la Loubère (1969: 124) again, "there hardly is a *Siamese* rich enough to build a Temple, who does it not...," even though there were not enough monks to fill them (Krom Sinlapakon 1969: 106). Judging by the Bangkok era, each family of substance "owned" a temple *(cao-khong wat)* where they cremated their dead, enshrined their ashes, and let their children play. The greater a family's wealth and power, the richer its temple was, and the richest might win the honor of royal patronage. Here, as at Sukhothai, we see display born of rivalry creating a gift-centered Buddhism. When displaying status carried such high stakes, how can Buddhism's other status-denying options—asceticism, meditation, and ethical deeds—have stood a chance?

Why Buddhism?: Status demanded display, but it did not have to be as Buddhist gifts. Khmer kings built resthouses and hospitals. A Tai lord might build a spirit shrine or enlarge his palace, sponsor a Brahmanical rite, or bring artists into his court. Indeed, the Tai elite did all of these things, but such displays were overshadowed by, and often incorporated in, their Buddhist gift-giving. Why was Buddhism the favored idiom of display?

Sukhothai and Ayutthaya suggest differing answers. For Sukhothai, Buddhism promised centralization and consolidation. Its hierarchy by "merit" not only made a single elite possible, it undercut petty lords whose rule rested on "blood" and, perhaps, links to local spirits. Of course Sukhothai's rulers may not have seen this clearly—perhaps they were only making allies in an age when charismatic monks wielded great power—but then their experiences in trying to create a polity above lesser ones must have made them ready to hear Buddhism's universalizing message. Certainly Lüthai, and perhaps earlier kings, staked a Buddhist claim to rule, and so the monarch had to favor Buddhist displays.

Ayutthaya did not need such Buddhaization. Once it had triumphed over local elites, making their lords into commoners or courtiers, Buddhist universalism may have done less to help integrate the polity than impose ethical constraints on the king's rule. Anyway, the throne's dilemma was not to create but control an elite. To this end, laws specified everyone's rights and honors. Sumptuary laws restricted many displays to what the king granted. That should have made a well-ordered elite, but we know that manpower and trade opened opportunities for the ambitious to get more than the king gave. Once one had more, rivalry demanded display. Yet the wrong display was dangerous if it outdid the king or claimed a dignity he had not granted. So, as la Loubère (1969: 51, 69) says, people took pains to hide their wealth lest the king confiscate it. Of course he also says everyone rich enough to afford a temple built one— and that tells us the one route for the upwardly mobile. Buddhist gift-giving was the one approved way to display great wealth. After all, as a Buddhist monarch and the patron of religion, the king could not restrict merit-making. Besides, he had no reason to see such displays as a challenge. As an inscription from 1510 tells us, the merit of great gifts could be dedicated to the king (Griswold and Prasert 1974b), and we know from the Bangkok era that he could direct offerings to suit his own ends and honor (O'Connor 1978: 178-188). Therefore, Sukhothai and Ayutthaya's differing routes reached the same point: a Buddhism that emphasized gift-giving.

Conclusion

When we look at other cultures and earlier eras, our first questions come from our present ideology. And so, our age asks about trade in ways that assume its significance. We eagerly ask "How much?" and "Who traded what with whom?" This is all well worth knowing, but it hides more fundamental questions like "What was trade?"; "Did trade matter?"; or even "Why trade?" I wish this paper had answered these basic questions, but the best I can say is that it has posed them. To conclude, let me first try to address each of these questions, and then explore why Buddhism had affinities with trade.

What Was Trade?: We have tried to answer this question by saying where trade fit within the culture. If our first impulse would be to put trade in the economy, we find that the polity subsumed what we would call the economy. Petty dealings might follow the market's principles, but as their scale grew they became political and thus subject to a different set of principles. This suggests a continuum, and indeed the Tai word (*kankha, kha-khai*) will do for dealings big or small. In itself, this link to the bottom helps explain trade's stigma at the top of society. It also questions our focus on the top and, without other sources, makes it impossible to say just what trade was. Whatever the answer, trade was not one thing but many. Whether one looks at the top-to-bottom continuum or how at the top trade ran from gifts to tribute, compulsory trade and near plunder, it is clear that what we would call trade had many varieties. Of course we would expect that when trade had to operate by the polity's rather than its own principles.

Did Trade Matter?: Surely it mattered to the traders, but our question really asks if it changed society. As an autonomous entity, trade can act powerfully on society. Yet for the Tai that entity dissolves once put in context and that saps much of its power. True, trade was still potent enough to change Tai life, but not as the prime mover. If we play the game of splitting apart the "threefold union"—trade, empire, and Buddhism—then the polity was prior. Its pattern, emboxment, preceded trade; the first great Tai polity, Sukhothai, arose without extensive trade; and throughout the era studied the polity set the conditions wherein trade was possible. Of course within this study we have seen how at Ayutthaya trade became a major centralizing force that may have provoked recurrent crises.

Why Trade?: That sounds like a stupid question because we think we know the answer: self-interest. Yet that is not an answer, it is an article of faith. In this paper I have tried to go deeper to show how the elite's interests in trading varied according to the polity's structure and their religion. To begin with, the polity, rule, and status required wealth. That gave all Tai elites a reason to trade, but this was offset by trade's stigma and its potential to disrupt society. Given this balance, the polity's structure became decisive. When it fomented competition within the elite, their reason to trade grew. This reasoning puts the polity first and trade second. Was trade ever first, creating a polity to suit itself? We cannot deny that trade altered Ayutthaya's elite and intensified rivalry, but the larger political structure had other origins. After all, Ayutthaya established itself first militarily, and major trade came only later. Once it came, it may indeed have helped the center institute further status distinctions, but it never instituted a trade-centered polity. As with all Tai polities, manpower remained key.

Add Buddhism and that gave status rivalry what it needed to flourish: an ever-open, always-valued idiom for display. Why did Buddhism's many possibilities solidify into a gift-giving style? For

48

Sukhothai, tribute and booty must have made gifts a measure of prowess, but our best guess is that this style fits the polity's overriding need to make many local elites into one ruling class. Certainly this Siamese style antedates major trade. Ramkamhaeng's emphasis on the *kathin* tells us that much. For Ayutthaya, however, trade wealth surely strengthened any gift-giving proclivities. And so, apparently first the polity and then trade shaped the Siamese style of Buddhism.

This puts Buddhism second and makes it passive, but in many other ways it was prior and active. Let me begin with the obvious. Major trade arose in major polities. Buddhism not only made large realms plausible by depicting a world of great kings and glorious cities, it made them possible by eroding localism and providing an ideology and rituals for kingship. Therefore, as the polity's partner, Buddhism made opportunities for trade to grow.

Yet the size of trade probably mattered less than its cultural "place," and here Buddhism by itself gave trade a new location. If, as we have argued, trade stood outside of early Tai society, then Buddhism put it inside within what was now lay life. How? Buddhism constructed a radically new outside—monasticism. In Buddhist eyes, kings, farmers and, yes, even merchants were all alike—lay people mired in suffering. True, that did not put trade within the familial "box"—this tension remained—but it made a wider society where merchants had a place. Trade was not only more acceptable but more plausible. Now, if this symbolic shift seems too abstract to matter—even though it is no more abstract than talking about an economy or Tai society—we should note that, again and again, well-known Buddhist texts included merchants within society, sometimes as great supporters of the Buddha. Rituals did the same, lumping merchants with the other laity and setting them all apart from the monks. Thus, the Tai had to get the message, and trade got a new place.

Buddhism also "opened up" the Tai world view in a way that made room for trade. Earlier, following Hocart (1970: ch. 6) and Boon (1983), we noted how Buddhism created new needs. Unlike earlier religions that stopped when they got "life," Buddhism's quest for the "good" knew no end. We have already given clues that this increased ritual costs, but the larger point is that it went beyond ritual. Earlier religions treated ritual pragmatically, a mere means to an end; but, as monasticism shows, Buddhism made ritual a paradigm for living. True, not everyone could live as a monk, but rituals showed them how they were supposed to live. Earlier religions did not and could not conceive of this. They worked upon an existing life; they did not proclaim a better one. When they joined male and female symbols, it was not a model for living but of life. Besides, in life a person is male or female, high or low, left or right. One sought balance, not to be all of these at once. Against this dualism, complete in itself, Buddhism posited a single principle to which one could dedicate a ritual or a life. Instead of balance, one could now want perfection or progress. Of course most Tai ended up somewhere between the old and new religion, seeking balance yet wanting betterment, but any combination still opened up new possibilities. Once betterment was possible, people could want more. That made it easier for some to turn to trade and others to frequent the market. To put this more broadly, where economies were largely embedded, trade needed this more open world to flourish.

Again, perhaps a more open world seems too abstract. To be concrete and quite literal, note that many local rituals required closure of Tai and other Southeast Asian villages (MacDonald 1957). To achieve balance—equilibrium—one needed boundaries. Obviously this impeded trade, but it did not matter much in itself. What mattered more was that such rituals helped to create closed societies. In contrast, Buddhist rituals for the laity often defined a center—a monk, relic, or image—but left the peripheries open.[33] Indeed, the *kathin* is customarily made by one village to another village's temple, making it the antithesis of the earlier religion's rituals of village closure. Therefore, even these particulars fit the larger pattern: Buddhism and trade had many affinities.

Buddhism and Trade—Why Affinity?: Like any historical religion, Buddhism bore the marks of its birth. It was, as Weber (1967: 204-205) noted, an urban religion. And so, merchants, markets, and trade were part of the picture from the first. Naturally they appeared in the texts. Understandably, they shaped Buddhist thought, if only by defining the lay life monasticism rejected. As offspring of the same era, Buddhism and trade had to have some affinities.

When we look at this era, a far deeper reason for their affinities appears: Buddhism was an adaptation to a world of trade and empire. Like other prophetic world religions, Buddhism arose in an era of crisis. Empires and trade had remade, or perhaps we should say undone, the world, leaving life out of wack with religion. Enter the Buddha to bring them back together again. How? As a prophet his vision had coherence (Weber 1964: 58-59). It came fresh from a single man, free of the old religion's crust of compromise. Yet it went further to shed all of this world's particularism and proclaim a higher universal order. This development was not unique to the Buddha. Jesus Christ and Mohammed faced similar crises and, as Peacock and Kirsch (1980; also see Bellah 1964) show, took the same evolutionary step: radically devaluing this world to posit a higher reality.

Once ultimate reality left the everyday world, religion stood above its vagaries, and ordinary life could change more freely. After all, now what really mattered stood outside of life. If trade, empires, and cities set the stage for this epochal change, they could not pull it off. Their piecemeal changes could undo the world, but only a prophet could put it back together again. Yet once religion had reordered the world, trade and rule could prosper in new ways. Their potential coherence had to await a more universalized world.

Turning to the Tai, we find a far different sequence. The solution preceded the problem. Before merchants and rulers had fully undone the world, Buddhism was there remaking it in ways suited to their growth. It is in this sense that we say Buddhism opened the Tai for trade. If in India Buddhism was first an adaptation to this new world, for the Tai it was a preadaptation, an architect making the new world possible.

To conclude, let me put all of this in the perspective of Southeast Asia where trade, Indic religions, and the first cities went together. Scholars sometimes speak of primary urbanization where cities arise from native roots as opposed to secondary urbanization where they come from borrowings. By these standards, Southeast Asia was a region of secondary urban genesis. However true this may be, it tells us very little and ignores the Southeast Asian city's deep indigenous roots (O'Connor 1983). We might do better to speak of secondary religious evolution where borrowed Indic religions recreated a world suited to trade and empire.

Acknowledgments

An earlier version of this paper was presented at the Southeast Asian Studies Summer Institute Conference in DeKalb, Illinois, July 31, 1986, and later, after substantial revision, at the Association for Asian Studies meetings in Boston, April 10, 1987. Many people have made helpful comments. I am particularly indebted to Kenneth Hall, Nicola Tannenbaum, F. K. Lehman, and Lucien Hanks.

NOTES

1. Consider the Tai Deng who say that the house of their lord or *tao (cao)* is like that of their mother and father (Robert 1941: 26), and whose proverbs urge 'love' *(rak)* between ruler and ruled as well as within the family (Degeorge 1927-1928). Gedney (1964: 47) observes that in Tai Deng and several other Tai dialects a word for king is cognate with a verb meaning "'to care for (a sick person)' and sometimes 'to protect'." For tribal Tai, Tomosugi (1980: 106) notes how casting the ruler-ruled relationship in kin terms "indicates that the norm of dominance and subordination was not separable from the underlying norm of reciprocity...." For Tai Yuan peasants, Turton (1978: 126) notes how some obligations to the state are phrased in the idiom of respect used for parents and elders. See Condominas (1980) for a more complete picture of the non-Buddhist and, by inference, pre-Buddhist Tai.

2. This state of affairs is a clash in expectation and ideology, not necessarily the realities of trade and rule. The "inside" denied or at least hid what the "outside" accepted. Where this failed, boundaries between "in" and "out" shifted (O'Connor 1986b).

3. This concept applies to the elite, and even then Tai peoples varied in their attitude towards trade. Among Lü and northeastern Tai villagers, successful traders won respect (Moerman 1975; Keyes 1977: 147), but they could hardly match the Shan among whom perhaps a quarter engaged in trade (Scott 1932: 205). At the opposite extreme, Siamese villagers relegated most trade to ethnic minorities (Ingram 1971: 19-20) while their elite depended on trade to support the court.

4. As Weber (1968: 21) says, "Charismatic political heroes seek booty....But charisma...always rejects as undignified any pecuniary gain that is methodical and rational."

5. As these societies stress status, following Bourdieu (1977), one might argue that strategy or praxis appears as power. As Wolfe (1977: 162) says, "Violence is the simple, ultimate solution for problems of status competition...."

6. For a Siamese example, consider how Kemp (1984: 64) puts 19th century patron-client ties on a continuum. At one end (what we would call the "outside"), formal patron-client bonds "were concerned with the exercise of explicit power and authority...." At the other end stood kinship (the idiom of the "inside"), which was the formal bond's opposite, "perhaps not always in practice but certainly so in terms of its moral structure...." This recalls Hanks' (1962) point that "power" is amoral and "merit" moral efficacy.

7. See, for example, the myth of Queen Chammathewi and the Lawa ruler (Kraisri 1967) and the extensive works of Archaimbault (1973) on Lao royal ritual.

8. For example, compared to the Siamese, the Shan show far greater concern for an amoral power quite apart from merit (see Tannenbaum n.d., to Hanks 1962). Their stress on keeping Buddhist precepts (Tannenbaum n.d.) differs from the Siamese emphasis on merit-making, a subject considered below. For the Lao village, Taillard (1977: 78-80) argues that there is an opposition between merit (*boun*) and *piep*, a pre-Buddhist, competitive way to assert one's strength and claim prestige. While this is not simply merit and power, it would almost certainly be an aspect of the Lao status-power configuration.

9. For simpler societies, this accords with Hutterer's (1985: 3-4) view that external trade had to be institutionalized. For a more complex society, consider India where Dumont (1970: 166) says "it was only in periods of political unification and large and fairly well policed kingdoms that the king was able to concern himself with the kingdom's prosperity and promote trade for his own interests."

10. If that is common to many peoples, it was especially significant to the Tai for whom hierarchy within society is often predicated on the perceived order of the outside world (such as, the upland Tai lords borrow from the Vietnamese, the Tai Yuan from the Mon and later Burmese, the Siamese and Lao from the Khmer, and today all Tai elites borrow from the West to affirm their status).

11. Compare Leach (1965: 215) and Scott (1932: 205) on the Shan with Chen (1949: 54-60) on the Lü. On trade in general, note that "The Yunnan Tai (which includes the Lü) do not...trade on as large a scale as the Shan Tai in Burma" (Lebar 1964: 208-209). This contrast suggests that Chinese influence on the Lü elite may enter into the Lü-Shan difference. Similarly, the Vietnamese have influenced the White and Black Tai elites who also do not favor trade. If these Sino-Vietnamese influences included a disdain for trade, then that could provide an alternative to our thesis that ascribed status discouraged trade. Yet it could also support our thesis in that as overlords the Chinese and Vietnamese buttressed existing Tai elites so that they did not have to achieve their status.

12. Some have argued that Ramkamhaeng established a pottery industry, but Hein, Burns and Richards (1985) have found archaeological evidence suggesting a much older ceramic tradition.

13. In this and following references to inscriptions, the Roman numeral indicates the face and the following Arabic numerals the line on that face of the inscription.

14. See Weber (1967: 260, 376 fn. 16) where he says "the administration strove to break the power of the presumably feudal-notables."

15. Did these policies apply to all the *muang* in his realm or just his own immediate *muang*? Either way the policy undermined rival lords—the question is simply which lords. His grandson, Lüthai, faced the same problem, but in this instance it is clear that these policies do apply to all of the *muang* in the realm. In Inscription 3 he essentially repeats his grandfather's policy, "gives the vassal rulers a stiff lecture" on abiding by it (II/34-47), and then lists sites in his own and vassal

muang where he has put this inscription (Griswold and Prasert 1973: 86).

16. Certainly Sukhothai never categorically made the center-defining status distinctions that institutionalized Ayutthaya's pre-eminence. Thus, even in Lüthai's inscriptions Sukhothai is still a *muang* (such as in Inscription 3, I/4, Griswold and Prasert 1973), not something different and superior to the lesser *muang* that composed it (but perhaps *ban muang* at II/30 was a beginning); and while in one passage he could distinguish vassal lords from independent ones (*cao* vs. *cao pen khun*, II/16-23), a few lines later when he lectures his vassals he uses the title for an independent lord *(khun)* and even grants some the respect of addressing them as his elders! Of course Ayutthaya consolidated its rule by making more precise distinctions, applying them to *muang* and not just lords but everyone (the *sakdina* system).

17. See for example Inscription 38 where the Ayutthaya king is referred to as *phra-ong than* and *phracao phaendin* as distinct from *chao ban* and *chao muang*; and Inscription 40 where he is *Somdet Caophraya*, which is clearly above the Sukhothai ruler who is a *phraya*, a title the ruler of almost any *muang* might claim (Griswold and Prasert 1969, 1970).

18. While Sukhothai was a Khmer outpost, it was not a cultural center such as Lopburi. Apparently Sukhothai's elite did not make the heavy expenditures on religion (monuments, images) that at Lopburi testify to status competition.

19. In the *Kotmai Tra Sam Duang* (1963) laws governing Ayutthaya's markets stress the need to control theft.

20. Why could the king control land and trade more readily than manpower? If, as seems probable, the Tai expansion capitalized on existing manpower institutions, then we would expect earlier, more "tribal" rights to be preserved in the new kingdoms. In contrast, Tai who immigrated had to give up local trade and land rights, making it easier for their newly powerful leaders to claim these in the new polity.

21. Where Tambiah (1970: 337) sees four clearly structured systems in his northeastern village, Textor (1973: 31-32) says these "would be inappropriate to the very different, generally less clearly structured situation one meets in Bang Chan." One would expect this situation if Tambiah's village emphasized the oppositions of the old religion as opposed to Bang Chan's more Buddhaized world.

22. A hint of how Buddhism opposed this appears in Inscription 13 where, in a list of deeds whose merit was dedicated to the king, it says the ruler prohibited selling cattle to the Lawa (Griswold and Prasert 1974b). Lawa were autochthonous people, and so it seems probable that they practiced the cattle sacrifice common to the uplands. Griswold and Prasert suggest they were butchers.

23. Legitimacy from ruler to ruled went through individual patron-client ties. Such ties cannot have legitimated *the* elite but only particular leaders to particular followers.

24. For the past, contrast mid-14th century Siamese inscriptions (discussed below) with the more precept-oriented Tai Yuan inscription of 1370 (Griswold and Prasert 1974a). It extols one monk's ability to get ill-doers to observe the precepts (I/19) and even goes so far as to note the quite obvious fact that those who were ordained observed the precepts (I/32-33).

25. Tannenbaum (1987) notes that the most powerful Shan tattoos oblige one to keep certain precepts. Their Siamese analogue, amulets, require respect, not precepts. Overall, as Tannenbaum shows, the Shan religious configuration differs markedly from the Siamese. In particular, it appears that the Shan separation of precept-linked power from merit is quite distinct from the Siamese proclivity for joining merit and power. This attitude suggests the greater importance of merit-making—and thus gift-giving—for the Siamese.

26. Of course Kingshill is right not to make too much of the actual words, but the difference becomes a bit more significant when we consider Ramkamhaeng's late 13th century inscription where he refers to the holy day as *wan suat tham* (III/16), the 'day for chanting the Dhamma,' or as Griswold and Prasert (1971: 214) say, 'day for preaching.' Either way this distinction stresses monastic activity, not lay asceticism.

27. Kaempfer's (1977: 21-22) account from the late 17th century says there were "several yearly solemn festivals," but he also stresses *songkran* and *kathin*, dividing the latter into water and land ceremonies. He mentions two "others"—an annual washing of the [royal?] elephants' heads and the beginning and end of lent.

28. Of course the Lao held *kathin*, but Reynolds (1978) seems correct in leaving it out of the key state rituals. It might be better to compare the Siamese stress on the *kathin* to the very popular Lao *boun phra vet* ceremony (indeed, Condominas 1968: 119, says this usage outdoes the

kathin in rural Laos). Both stress gift-giving, but where the Siamese ceremony *makes* a substantial gift, the Lao one only *commemorates* the great gifts the Buddha made in one birth as a prince.

To complete our comparison we should note that the other key Lao state ceremony, the New Year's lustration of the monks, had some Siamese parallels. Going by Reynolds' (1978: 170) interpretation that this rite stresses the Sangha, then it is analogous to the Siamese *kathin* (without the major gifts) as well as the apparently less significant annual rite of royally sponsored ordination (*buat nak luang,* Damrong 1967: 266). If, on the other hand, we consider that the Lao lustration of monks from the city's temples of the four quarters was intended to exorcise evil, then the Siamese held a parallel rite in the fourth month (Damrong 1967: 269-270). Yet it is improbable that this rite was as important to the Siamese as it was to the Lao. Very briefly, we can say that rites of fertility required boundaries and allowed closure, while monistic rites emphasized the center and opened up communities to the outside.

29. Competition in asceticism probably focused in the Sangha and in particular pitted the forest monks against the town monks (Tambiah 1984). While the forest monks were often more rigorous in their asceticism, they did not always have the favor of the urban-centered, status-conscious elite (O'Connor 1978: 149-151).

30. If Lüthai's Sukhothai was far wealthier than in his grandfather's day, one might argue that this was an equivalent gift, but I know of nothing that indicates a comparable increase in wealth. Where Ramkamhaeng's gift apparently totaled two million cowries, Lüthai's included ten million cowries, probably 5,000 ounces each of gold and silver and much more (Griswold and Prasert 1971: 209 fn. 65; 1973: 141 fn. 44, 158).

31. Instead of stressing asceticism, Lüthai says "everyone should be assiduous in doing homage to stupas, cetiyas and srimahabodhi trees" and that if done in perfect faith the worshiper would be reborn in heaven to await the coming of the next Buddha (Inscription 3, I/56-63, Griswold and Prasert 1973:102-104). Such worship almost certainly meant a gift, however small (incense, flowers). Obviously, it did not preclude asceticism, but consider Sadler's (1970: 282-284) argument that Burmese lay Buddhism divides into a monastery side that encourages lay asceticism, and a shrine side that stresses gifts and rituals' "grace-giving encounter with the holy." Elsewhere I have argued that physically and symbolically this monastery-shrine split held in Sukhothai (O'Connor 1985b). All of this suggests that Lüthai's stress on shrines emphasized gift-giving instead of lay asceticism. Granted, Lüthai did ordain temporarily, but this emphasized monastic

asceticism and in itself did not encourage lay asceticism as the way to make merit. Conversely, the ordination ceremony stresses how lay gifts permit monastic asceticism. Stressing this division of labor cannot have encouraged lay asceticism.

32. See Kirsch's (1984) observations on Mengrai and my comments on monks replacing petty lords (O'Connor 1985b).

33. Unlike lay rituals, monastic rituals that are formal acts of the Sangha (*sangkhakam*) do require boundaries. Oddly enough, this requirement is due to the Sangha being so open. Unless a specific chapter is specified, the Sangha includes all monks everywhere in the line of the Buddha. As passing a formal act requires consensus, usually boundary stones are used to define the Sangha (that is, a specific chapter). Significantly, the king must grant the land marked off by the boundary stones, thus ensuring that ritually complete chapters have a tie to the outside. Of course, ordination lines and teacher-pupil bonds also link monks to the world beyond the village. Indeed, given that all ordinations must be traced back to the Buddha's India, the Sangha is an intrinsically supra-local institution.

References

Abbreviations

BEFEO—*Bulletin de l'Ecole francaise d'Extrême-Orient*
EHS—*Epigraphic & Historical Studies*
JSS—*Journal of the Siam Society*

Abadie, M.
1924.   *Les races du Haut-Tonkin de Phong-Tho à Lang-Son.*   Paris: Société d'éditions géographiques, maritimes et coloniales.

Archaimbault, C.
1959a.   "La naissance du monde selon le bouddhisme siamois." In *La naissance du monde.* Paris: Editions du Seuil.

1959b.   "La naissance du monde selon les traditions lao: le mythe de Khun Bulom." In *La naissance du monde.* Paris: Editions du Seuil.

1964.   "Religious Structures in Laos. " *JSS* 52(1): 57-74.

1973.   *Structures religieuses lao (Rites et mythes).*   Vientiane: Vithagna.

1975.   "Le sacrifice du buffle à l'Autel du T'at Luong (Wieng Can)."
         Ethnos 40(1-4): 114-149.

Bellah, R.
1964.   "Religious Evolution." *American Sociological Review* 29: 358-374.

Bonifacy, A.
1915.   "Le fête Tay du Hô-Bô." *BEFEO* 15(3): 17-23.

Boon, J.
1983.   "Incest Recaptured: Some Contraries of Karma in Balinese
         Symbology." In *Karma: An Anthropological Inquiry*, edited by
         C. F. Keyes and E. V. Daniel, 185-222. Berkeley: University of
         California Press.

Bourdieu, P.
1977.   *Outline of a Theory of Practice*. New York: Cambridge
         University Press.

Chamberlain, J. R.
1986.   "Remarks on the Origins of Thao Hung or Cheuang." In *Papers
         from a Conference on Thai Studies in Honor of William J.
         Gedney*, edited by R. J. Bickner, T. J. Hudak, and Patcharin
         Peyasantiwong, 57-90. Ann Arbor: University of Michigan
         Center for South and Southeast Asian Studies.

Charnvit Kasetsiri
1976.   *The Rise of Ayudhaya: A History of Siam in the Fourteenth and
         Fifteenth Centuries*. Kuala Lumpur: Oxford University Press.

Chen Han-seng
1949.   *Frontier Land Systems in Southernmost China*. New York:
         Institute of Pacific Relations.

Coedès, G.
1954.   "L'art siamois de l'Époque de Sukhodaya." *Arts Asiatiques* 1(4):
         281-302.

Condominas, G.
1968.   "Notes sur le Bouddhisme populaire en milieu rural lao."
         Archives de Sociologie des Religions 13(25): 81-110; 13(26): 111-
         150.

1980.   *L'espace social à propos de l'asie de sud-est*. Paris: Flammarion.

Damrong Rajanubhab, Prince (compiler)
1967.   *Khamhaikan caokrungkao*. Bangkok: Khlangwitthaya.

Dang Nghiem Van
1972.   "An Outline of the Thai in Viet Nam." *Vietnamese Studies* 32: 143-196.

Davis, R. B.
1984.   *Muang Metaphysics: A Study of Northern Thai Myth and Ritual.* Bangkok: Pandora.

Degeorge, J-B.
1927-8.   "Proverbes, maximes et sentences Tays." *Anthropos* 22: 911-32; 23: 596-616.

Dumont, L.
1970.   *Homo Hierarchicus.* Chicago: University of Chicago Press.

Durkheim, E.
1964.   *The Division of Labor in Society.* New York: Free Press.

Durrenberger, E. Paul
1980.   "Annual non-Buddhist Religious Observances of Mae Hong Son Shan." *JSS* 68(2): 48-56.

Foster, B. G.
1982.   *Commerce and Ethnic Differences: The Case of the Mons in Thailand.* Athens: Ohio University Center for International Studies, Southeast Asia Program.

Gedney, W. J.
1964.   "A Comparative Sketch of White, Black and Red Thai." *Social Science Review* 1 (Special Issue): 1-47.

Geertz, C.
1980.   *Negara: The Theatre State in Nineteenth-Century Bali.* Princeton: Princeton University Press.

Gosling, E.
1983.   "History of Sukhothai as a Ceremonial Center: A Study of Early Siamese Architecture and Society." Ph.D. dissertation, University of Michigan.

Griswold, A.B. and Prasert na Nagara
1969.   "A Law Promulgated by the King of Ayudhya in 1397 A.D." *EHS* no. 4, *JSS* 57(1): 109-149.

1970.   "A Pact between Uncle and Nephew." *EHS* no. 5, *JSS* 58(1): 89-113.

1971.   "The Inscription of King Rama Gamheng of Sukhodaya (1292 A.D.)." *EHS* no. 9, *JSS* 59(2): 179-228.

1973. "The Epigraphy of Mahadharmaraja I of Sukhodaya." *EHS* no. 11, Pt. 1, *JSS* 61(1): 71-179.

1974a. "The Inscription of Wat Pra Yun." *EHS* no. 13, *JSS* 62(1): 123-141.

1974b. Inscription of the Siva of Kamben Bejra. *EHS* no. 14, *JSS* 62(2): 223-238.

Hall, K. R.
1985. *Maritime Trade and State Development in Early Southeast Asia.* Honolulu: University of Hawaii Press.

Hanks, J. R.
1960. "Reflections on the Ontology of Rice." In *Culture in History: Essays in Honor of Paul Radin,* edited by S. Diamond, 298-301. New York: Columbia University Press.

Hanks, L. M.
1962. "Merit and Power in the Thai Social Order." *American Anthropologist* 64: 1247-1261.

Hein, D., P. Burns and D. Richards
1985. "An Alternative View on the Origins of Ceramic Production at Sisatchanalai and Sukhothai, Thailand." Paper presented to the SPAFA Technical Workship on Ceramics, Thailand, December 2-10.

Heitzman, J.
1984. "Early Buddhism, Trade and Empire." In *Studies in the Archaeology and Palaeoanthropology of South Asia,* edited by K. A. R. Kennedy and G. L. Possehl, 121-137. New Delhi: American Institute of Indian Studies.

Hocart, A. M.
1970. *Kings and Councillors.* Chicago: University of Chicago Press.

Hutterer, K.
1985. "A Balance of Trade: The Social Nature of Late Pre-Hispanic Philippines." Hart Collection Lecture. Northern Illinois University.

Ingram, J. C.
1971. *Economic Change in Thailand 1850-1970.* Stanford: Stanford University Press.

Kaempfer, E.
1977. "Ayuthaya and Siam." In *Southeast Asia and the Germans.* Tubingen: Horst Erdmann Verlag.

Kemp, J. H.
1984.   "The Manipulation of Personal Relations: From Kinship to
          Patron-clientage."   In *Strategies and Structures in Thai Society*,
          edited by H. Bummelhuis and J. Kemp, 55-69.   Amsterdam:
          Vakgroep Zuid- en Zuidoost-Azië, Universiteit van Amsterdam.

Keyes, C. F.
1977.   *The Golden Peninsula: Culture and Adaptation in Mainland
          Southeast Asia*. New York: Macmillan.

1983.   "Merit-transference in the Karmic Theory of Popular Theravada
          Buddhism." In *Karma: An Anthropological Inquiry*, edited by C.
          F. Keyes and E. V. Daniel, 261-289.   Berkeley: University of
          California Press.

Kingshill, K.
1960.   *Ku Daeng—The Red Tomb: A Village Study in Northern
          Thailand*. Chiang Mai: Prince Royal's College.

Kirsch, A. Thomas
1977.   "Complexity in the Thai Religious System: An Interpretation."
          Journal of Asian Studies 36(2): 241-266.

1984.   "Cosmology and Ecology as Factors in Interpreting Early Thai
          Social Organization." *Journal of Southeast Asian Studies* 15(2):
          253-265.

Kotmai Tra Sam Duang
1963.   [The Laws of the Three Seals]. Bangkok: Khurusapha.

Kraisri Nimmanahaeminda
1967.   "The Romance of Khun Luang Viranga." *Sawaddi* 5(4): 8-10, 22-
          24.

Krom Sinlapakon
1969.   *Ruang krungkao.   Prachum phongsawadan*, pt. 63, vol. 37.
          Bangkok: Khurusapha.

Lach, Donald F.
1965.   *Asia in the Making of Europe*. Chicago: University of Chicago
          Press, vol. 1.

la Loubère, Simon de
1969.   *The Kingdom of Siam*. London: Oxford University Press.

Leach, E. R.
1965.   *Political Systems of Highland Burma*. Boston: Beacon Press.

Lebar, F. L., G. C. Hickey, and J. K. Musgrave
1964. *Ethnic Groups of Mainland Southeast Asia.* New Haven: Human Relations Area Files.

Low, Lt. Col. J.
1847. "On the Laws of Muung Thai or Siam." *Journal of the Indian Archipelago and Eastern Asia* 1: 328-426.

Lüthai, King
1982. *Three Worlds According to King Ruang: A Thai Buddhist Cosmology.* Translated by F. E. and M. B. Reynolds. Berkeley: Berkeley Buddhist Studies Series 4.

MacDonald, A. W.
1957. "Notes sur la claustration villageoise dans l'Asie du Sud-Est." *Journal Asiatique* 245: 185-210.

Maspero, Henri
1950. "La société et la religion des Chinois anciens et celles des Thai modernes." In *Les Religions Chinoises,* 139-211. Paris: Civilisations du Sud SAEP.

Moerman, M.
1966. "Ban Ping's Temple: The Center of a Loosely Structured Society." In *Anthropological Studies in Theravada Buddhism,* edited by M. Nash, 137-174. Southeast Asian Cultural Report, no. 13. New Haven: Yale University.

1975. "Chiangkham's Trade in the 'Old Days'." In *Change and Persistence in Thai Society: Essays in Honor of Lauriston Sharp,* edited by G. W. Skinner and A. T. Kirsch, 151-171. Ithaca: Cornell University Press.

Mus, P.
1975. *India Seen from the East: Indian and Indigenous Cults in Champa.* Translated by I. W. Mabbett. Melbourne: Monash University Centre of Southeast Asian Studies.

O'Connor, R. A.
1978. "Urbanism and Religion: Community, Hierarchy and Sanctity in Urban Thai Buddhist Temples." Ph.D. dissertation, Cornell University.

1983. *A Theory of Indigenous Southeast Asian Urbanism.* Singapore: Institute of Southeast Asia Studies.

1985a. "Enduring Realities and Persistent Change in Early Southeast Asian Polities." Paper presented at the Association for Asian Studies meetings, Philadelphia, March 22.

1985b.   "Centers and Sanctity, Regions and Religion: Varieties of Tai Buddhism." Paper presented at the American Anthropological Association meetings, Washington, D.C., December 4-8.

1986a.   "Trade and the Tai." Paper presented at the Southeast Asian Studies Summer Institute Conference, Northern Illinois University, DeKalb, July 31.

1986b.   "Merit and the Market: Thai Symbolizations of Self-interest." *JSS* 74: 62-82.

Peacock, J. L. and A. T. Kirsch
1980.   *The Human Direction: An Evolutionary Approach to Social and Cultural Anthropology.* Third edition. Englewood Cliffs: Prentice Hall.

Peterson, J. T.
1977.   "Ecotones and Exchange in Northern Luzon." In *Economic Exchange and Social Interaction in Southeast Asia: Perspectives from Prehistory, History, and Ethnography,* edited by K. L. Hutterer, 55-71. Ann Arbor: University of Michigan Center for South and Southeast Asian Studies.

Reynolds, C. J.
1976.   "Buddhist Cosmography in Thai History, with Special Reference to Nineteenth-century Culture Change." *Journal of Asian Studies* 35(2): 203-220.

Reynolds, F. E.
1978.   "Ritual and Social Hierarchy: An Aspect of Traditional Religion in Buddhist Laos." In *Religion and Legitimation of Power in Thailand, Laos, and Burma,* edited by B. L. Smith, 166-174. Chambersburg: ANIMA.

1985.   "Theravada Buddhism and Economic Order." *Crossroads* 2(2): 61-82.

Robert, R.
1941.   *Notes sur les Tay Déng de lang chanh.* Hanoi: Institut Indochinois pour l'Étude de l'Homme, Mèmoire 1.

Sadler, A. W.
1970.   "Pagoda and Monastery: Reflections on the Social Morphology of Burmese Buddhism." *Journal of Asian and African Studies* 5(4): 282-293.

Scott, J. G.
1932.   *Burma and Beyond.* London: Grayson & Grayson.

Silvestre, Capitaine
1918.   "Les thai blancs de Phong-tho." *BEFEO* 18(4): 1-56.

Smith, B. (editor)
1978.   *Religion and Legitimation of Power in Thailand, Laos, and Burma.* Chambersburg: ANIMA.

Smith, G. V.
1977.   *The Dutch in Seventeenth-Century Thailand.* Special Report, no. 16. DeKalb: Center for Southeast Asian Studies.

1980.   "Princes, Nobles and Traders: Ethnicity and Economic Activity in Seventeenth-century Thailand." *Contributions to Asian Studies* 15: 6-14.

Taillard, C.
1977.   "Le village lao de la région de Vientiane: un pouvoir local face au pouvoir étatique." *L'Homme* 17(2-3): 71-100.

Tambiah, S. J.
1970.   *Buddhism and the Spirit Cults in North-east Thailand.* Cambridge: Cambridge University Press.

1976.   *World Conqueror and World Renouncer.* Cambridge: Cambridge University Press.

1984.   *The Buddhist Saints of the Forest and the Cult of Amulets.* Cambridge: Cambridge University Press.

Tannenbaum, N.
n.d.   "Shan Buddhism: Power, Protection, and Ethics." Manuscript.

1987.   "Tattoos: Invulnerability and Power in Shan Cosmology." *American Ethnologist* 14(4): 693-711.

Textor, R. B.
1973.   *Roster of the Gods.* New Haven: Human Relations Area Files.

"Thammachak" (pseud.)
1971.   *Anisong tang-tang.* Bangkok: Phitthayakhan.

Tomosugi, Takashi
1980.   *A Structural Analysis of Thai Economic History: Case Study of a Northern Chao Phraya Delta Village.* Tokyo: Institute of Developing Economies.

Trocki, C. A.
1979.   *Prince of Pirates.* Singapore: Singapore University Press.

Turton, A.
1978. "Architectural and Political Space in Thailand." In *Natural Symbols in South East Asia*, edited by G. B. Milner, 113-132. London: School of Oriental and African Studies.

Viraphol Sarasin
1977. *Tribute and Profit: Sino-Siamese Trade, 1652-1853*. Cambridge: Harvard University Press.

Weber, M.
1947. *The Theory of Social and Economic Organization*, translated by A. M. Henderson and T. Parsons, edited with an introduction by T. Parsons. New York: The Free Press.

1958. *From Max Weber*, Translated and edited by H. H. Gerth and C. Wright Mills. New York: Oxford University Press.

1964. *The Sociology of Religion*, translated by E. Fischoff. Boston: Beacon Press.

1967 (1958). *The Religion of India*, translated and directed by H. H. Gerth and Don Martindale. New York: The Free Press.

1968. *Max Weber on Charisma and Institution Building*, edited by S. N. Eisenstadt. Chicago: University of Chicago Press.

Wheatley, P.
1983. *Nagara and Commandery: Origins of the Southeast Asian Urban Traditions*. Chicago: Department of Geography, University of Chicago.

Witchitmatra
1973. *Prawat kankha Thai*. Bangkok: Ruamsan.

Wolfe, T.
1977. *Mauve Gloves and Madmen, Clutter and Vine*. New York: Bantam.

Wyatt, D. K.
1984. *Thailand: A Short History*. New Haven: Yale University Press.

POWER AND ITS SHAN TRANSFORMATIONS

Nicola Tannenbaum

It is my contention that the systematic variations
manifested by these groups [upland Southeast Asian
peoples] allows us to place them in a single analytical
model, and that they stem primarily from various
common features of the religious system. Some of these
common features include religious conceptions
regarding rewards for activities in this life which are
meted out in an after-life, ideas concerning human
"potency" and how it is acquired or manifested, and
ritual activities which must be performed to gain
"prestige" in this life as well as in a hereafter. (Kirsch
1973: 5)

Here Kirsch summarizes his basic argument that upland mainland
Southeast Asian societies express variations on the same theme of
power/potency. Durrenberger (1981b) argues that these variations in
political form result from differences in local ecological and economic
environments (see also Maran 1967; Lehman 1963). This ideological unity
exists in spite of the ethnic diversity in the highlands. Kirsch (1973) draws
primarily on accounts of Naga, Chin, Kachin, and Lamet peoples to
develop his argument. Durrenberger expands it with his analysis of Lisu.
Their analyses cut across major linguistic groups. Kirsch's argument and
Durrenberger's elaboration of it demonstrate the basic unity of upland
systems centered on the role of power/potency, productivity, how one
achieves it, and the necessity to publicly validate it through feasts and
generosity that increase the unit's power/potency.

The upland unity in world view raises the question of whether such a
unity also exists in the lowlands, and if it does, what its relationship is with
that in the highlands. Theravada Buddhism is often seen as providing the
underlying world view in these societies. Both inside and outside
observers identify these people as Buddhist and state that these societies
must be understood in Buddhist terms (Kirsch 1975, 1982, 1985; Reynolds
1977; Smith 1966; Spiro 1966, 1967, 1982; Tambiah 1970, 1976; Wells 1975;
Keyes 1971, 1984; Ebihara 1966; Lehman 1972; Nash 1966; Van Esterik
1982a, b; Rajavaramuni (Prayudh Payutto) 1984; Virasi n.d.; Umavijani n.d.;
Ramakomud 1985).

On the face of it, lowland societies appear to share an underlying
world view based on Theravada Buddhism rather than one based on
power/potency/fertility as in the uplands. Anthropological observers tend
to view lowland societies through Theravada Buddhist lenses (Kirsch 1977,
1982, 1985; Keyes 1984; Van Esterik 1982b; see also the sources cited

above). Nevertheless, Theravada Buddhism always appears with other religious practices (Spiro 1967)—the Hindu pantheon in Sri Lanka (Obeyesekere 1966; Ames 1966), nats in Burma (Spiro 1967; M. Nash 1966; J. Nash 1966), and the Hindu pantheon and assorted spirits in Thailand, Laos, and Cambodia (Kaufman 1960; Tambiah 1970; Durrenberger 1980; Archimbault 1959; deBerval 1959; and Ebihara 1966).

The relationship between Buddhist and animist practices has been a perduring problem in the analysis of lowland mainland Southeast Asian societies. These analyses fall into either of two broad perspectives: (1) Buddhism and animism serve two different functions with Buddhism as the dominant religion (Piker 1968; Ames 1966; Obeyesekere 1966; Blanchard 1958; Kirsch 1975; Klausner 1972; Tambiah 1970; Mendelson 1961a, b; and Van Esterik 1982a, b); or (2) Buddhism and animism are two separate and distinct religions (Spiro 1967, 1982; Boshe 1971; Ebihara 1966; Kaufman 1960; Graham 1912; Insor 1963; Landon 1949; Terwiel 1979; Htin 1962; and Condominas 1975). Regardless of how the relationship between Buddhism and animism is characterized, the problem of explaining the relationship remains. Focusing on Buddhism as the key and treating animist practices as secondary creates a false dichotomy between the two "systems." It becomes impossible to examine lowland religious systems as a unified whole, and, rather than analyses, one gets empty rhetoric over whether this or that practice is or is not Buddhist. I reject this approach and instead am concerned with the analysis of Shan world view, ideology, and religion. This perspective makes it possible to frame questions about continuities in upland and lowland societies and examine the relationship between religion, world view, and political economic form (Tannenbaum 1987; n.d.-a, n.d.-b).

The historical conjunction of these peoples, the evidence for a shared world view among upland peoples, and the existence of animist Tai groups suggest that there should be some continuities between uplanders and lowlanders. Yet, from a lowlander's perspective, upland and lowland people have nothing in common. Lowlanders phrase the contrast in terms of religion: they are Buddhists, the upland tribal peoples have no religion. This perception is based on the contrast between themselves as members of a state civilization and the upland peoples who live on the fringes of, but do not participate in, "civilization." The lowlanders' perception of themselves as members of states correctly identifies the main difference between upland and lowland peoples. This difference transforms the lowland world view in many ways.

States, as Fried (1967) argues, are the means of organizing and stabilizing social relationships when there is unequal access to basic productive resources or stratification. The "reality" of the lowland situation is that a small group of people controls access to resources. One expects an ideology that both justifies the distribution of power and resources but one that also helps obscure this "reality." Theravada

Buddhism with the law of karma—the inevitable consequences of actions both good and bad—provides a justification for the distribution of power. People in powerful positions are enjoying the benefits of past good deeds; poor people are reaping the consequences of past bad actions. When the lowlands became Buddhist, the people did not adopt all aspects of Buddhism. The elements of Buddhism that are important in practical religion are those that are compatible with or are in some way transformations of the basic Southeast Asian world view. Through time, the reality of stratification has modified both Buddhism and the underlying world view.

In the uplands, the ideology based on power, potency, and fertility fits well with either egalitarian or hierarchic organizations. In both these situations, every producing unit has access to basic productive resources; no one group controls access to land and labor, although in some situations founding groups may control access to more productive lands. There may be differences in peoples' status and prestige based on their productive success or their inherited predisposition for power/potency/fertility, but no one has a monopoly over such prestige and status.

Durrenberger (in this volume) provides a good account of the complex interrelationships among Lisu economics, politics, and ideology. He argues that access to hill fields for both rice and opium production and equal access to the market, plus the ideology centered on fertility/potency and the need to publicly validate those claims, result in an egalitarian formation. Limit access to markets or to the most productive lands and the system becomes hierarchic.

These different political forms rest on different ecological and economic bases. In the uplands, people grow crops in swidden fields. Yields are notoriously variable, depending on rainfall, soil fertility, and depredations by insects and other pests. This variation provides an unstable base for the development of long term claims to power and prestige. In the lowlands, irrigated rice provides a relatively stable and reliable source of rice. In mainland Southeast Asia, people generally have usufruct rights to land; a household has control over the fields its members have cleared and planted; when they no longer maintain the field, their rights lapse. This is true for both upland and lowland agriculture. However, because irrigated fields are seldom abandoned, they are not available to be reclaimed by others. It then becomes possible to inherit claims to irrigated fields. The stability of the population, predictable harvests, and the "ownership" of fields means that irrigated rice production provides the basis for a stable hierarchy and the development of stratification.

In this paper I argue that the structure shared by lowland societies is, in many ways, similar to that of the upland societies and that differences are a consequence of their radically different political and economic forms. My perspective differs from other scholars in that I focus on ideology and world view and use it to explain and interpret lowlanders' beliefs and practices, both animist and Buddhist. I frame this argument using Shan examples but expect that its general features are applicable to other lowland "Theravada Buddhist" societies.

The Shan

Shan are one of a number of minority groups in Thailand. Like lowland Thai, Lao, and Burmans, Shan are Theravada Buddhist. They support Buddhist temples and monks and observe Buddhist holy days. Shan live in the mountain valleys of southern China, the Shan States, and in Maehongson and Chiang Mai Provinces in Thailand. Like the other lowlanders, Shan have a long history of state organization (Moerman 1965; Mangrai 1981).

Shan in Maehongson Province are peasant farmers. They settled this area more than one hundred years ago, primarily from the Shan State of Mawk Mai, now part of Burma (Wilson 1985). They are now incorporated into the Thai state and have the same political administrative structure as the rest of Thailand. Local authorities, village headmen, and sub-district officers (Thai, *kamnan*), are likely to be Shan while the higher-ranking, centrally-appointed authorities are Central Thai. This differs from the historical past when they were ruled by Shan officials appointed by the Shan lord, *tsao pha*. While both the ruling personnel and the villagers' obligations to the state have changed, the villagers' subordinate position remains.[1]

Most householders make their living as farmers growing irrigated rice supplemented by swidden rice fields for subsistence, and sesame, soybeans, and garlic as cash crops (Durrenberger 1981a; Durrenberger and Tannenbaum 1983, in press; Tannenbaum 1982, 1984). In communities with access to mountains to make hill fields, even the poorest households are able to make fields; consequently few people are available to do wage work, and people solely dependent on wage work do not exist. In larger communities without access to hill fields, poor households must depend on wage work to augment their income from gardening activities or collecting and selling forest products.

Other village occupations are limited to storekeeping, mini-bus driving, or teaching. School teachers, usually from outside the village, are part of the Thai administration. In poor villages, storekeeping is likely to be a part-time occupation. Most communities are served by one or more mini-buses that provide transportation to the provincial capital of Maehongson. Mini-bus owners are wealthy, and the drivers tend to be relatives of the owners. Poor communities on the road are served by mini-buses based in wealthier nearby villages.

Shan, Burmans, Northern Thai, Lao, Central Thai, and Cambodians, all practice slightly different forms of Theravada Buddhism with slightly different festivals, different religious scripts, and different ordination lines. Nevertheless, they all identify themselves as Buddhist and recognize the others as their co-religionists.

Power in the Shan Context

For Shan, power *(haeng, takho)* is a basic, unquestioned part of the universe—it simply exists. However, it is not equally distributed throughout the universe; some beings have greater power, other beings less. All beings can be ranked in terms of their relative power. Spirits, as Kirsch (1973) suggests for upland societies, form one part of this continuum. In the lowlands, beings gain access to this power either through withdrawal and restraint or through taking refuge in more powerful others. Paradoxically, those beings most withdrawn from the world have the greatest power over worldly things.

Power implies protection. If one has access to power, one is protected; if one is protected, one has the power or freedom to do as one chooses. Hanks (1957) discusses Central Thai concepts of power and freedom in similar terms. Power/protection takes the form of barriers that ward off misfortune. Tattoos that protect from gunshot and knife wounds do so by surrounding the tattoo bearer's body with a protective barrier. The annual "repairing the village" *(mae waan)* ceremony closes off the village, drives dangerous beings out, and creates a barrier preventing these from entering the village (Tannenbaum n.d.-a).[2] Power/protection does not cause good things to happen; it is passive, merely preventing bad things from happening. The essence of power is its ability to ward off the consequences of behavior. Men with powerful anti-bullet and anti-knife tattoos are protected from retaliatory violence and are free to steal or kill without fear of the consequences.

Because the world is populated with powerful beings, many more powerful than any given human, it is necessary to enter into some kind of relationship with them to insure one's protection. Powerful beings are dangerous because they do not fear the consequences of their actions. They are free to behave as they choose and can easily be offended and cause harm. Villagers know this as part of existential reality. Offended spirits cause illnesses; offended government officials create real problems for villagers.

Beings with power/protection have the potential to withold it, leaving the person exposed to dangers from other beings. Consequently, powerful beings need to be treated circumspectly; the greater the being's power/protection, the greater the restraint in interaction. People deal with this power differential by limiting their interaction with powerful beings. Ordinary people do not often interact with monks or powerful government officials. Another method is to use an intermediary to interact with the powerful other on one's behalf. The *tsao muong*, the cadastral spirit and

"Lord of the Village," plays an important role in protecting the village. Villagers have an obligation to present him with offerings if they want to be included in this protection. However, because he is very powerful, villagers do not present these offerings themselves but instead give them to his intermediary, *phuu muong*, whose duty it is to present these offerings. The village headman serves a similar intermediary function in his relationship with more powerful government officials (Durrenberger 1981a; Tannenbaum n.d.-a).

Power derives automatically from the practice of austerities. The process is mechanical, and the practicer's morality or intentions do not affect the process. This is contrary to the standard Buddhist conception that people's intentions (Shan, *tsetana*) determine results. In Theravada Buddhist countries, practicing withdrawal and austerities, following Buddhist precepts (Shan, *sin;* Pali, *sila*), are considered equivalent to morality. Practicing morality, keeping precepts, is one way to gain merit. Precept-keeping automatically confers power; the more precepts one keeps, the greater one's power. Precept-keeping can be interpreted as either morality or power-seeking. The ambiguity lies not in the consequences of precept-keeping, which automatically convey power, but in people's motivations to do so. One can strive to keep precepts to aid in the escape from the cycle of rebirths, the approved motive, or one can do so to achieve magical power. Claiming mystical powers that one has not achieved is one of the four causes of expulsion from the monastic order. (The other three are killing or urging someone to kill another human, engaging in sexual intercourse, and stealing.) The automatic acquisition of mystical power is a recognized consequence of practicing restraint and withdrawal, but it is de-emphasized in scriptural Buddhism. The Buddha warns his followers not to be distracted from their goal of escaping the cycle of rebirths by the acquisition of mystical power. People's motivation for keeping precepts does not affect accumulation of power. Regardless of a man's intent when he becomes a monk, keeping the monastic precepts gives him great power and people interact with monks in the same way as other powerful beings.

Buddhas exemplify the peak of power; they have abandoned all worldly pleasures and demonstrate the power that can be achieved by such withdrawal. Monks keeping 227 precepts exemplify the most powerful beings with whom ordinary villagers can interact. Forest monks who practice additional austerities have greater power, and amulets made by these monks have great power. Ordinary men and women attempt to keep five precepts: to refrain from killing, stealing, improper sexual conduct, lying, and intoxication. However, they recognize that this level of restraint is difficult to achieve and only undertake to keep these on holy days.

Acquisition of power is not inherently connected with morality; yet it is easy to overlook the essential moral neutrality of power. Precept-

72

keeping is often glossed as the practice of morality (Spiro 1967, 1982). Buddhas and monks are seen as having power based on morality, or precept-keeping. Treating precept-keeping as the practice of morality is not wrong, since this is one possible interpretation, but it obscures the more basic fact that in this world view, restraint confers power.

Examining precept-keeping in a broader context illuminates the essentially moral neutrality of precept-keeping. People receiving powerful tattoos are required to keep one of the five everyday precepts at all times. If the person fails to keep the promised precept, the tattoo will not work, and, depending on the tattoo, the person will become physically or mentally ill. Typically the person takes the precept to refrain from improper sexual behavior, usually interpreted as refraining from adultery. By keeping this precept, a man with tattoos that protect him from gunshot wounds or knife cuts can rob and kill with impunity. Keeping this one precept does not imply any commitment to morality or right behavior; often, in fact, it suggests a commitment to a life of crime (Tannenbaum 1987).

A person making powerful tattoos and amulets must practice withdrawal and restraint or his tattoos and amulets will not be effective. The more precepts a person keeps, the greater his power, and the better he is able to draw on power from other sources. However, the recipient of the amulet or tattoos is not committed to restraint beyond keeping one precept (Tannenbaum 1987).

The Buddhas, their relics and teachings, and monks are all powerful objects in their own right. While it is possible to interpret these powerful beings and objects in Buddhist terms, there is more to power than Buddhism. It is a mistake to limit "Buddhist" objects to Buddhist interpretations. If one does so, one is either forced, like Spiro (1967, 1982), to develop separate analyses for animism and Buddhism or to dismiss the magical usages with the statement that they have scriptural support. Both approaches make it impossible to explain the magical usages. Tambiah's (1970) "elements in a religious field" does nothing more than recognize the coexistence of both magical and scriptural Buddhist practices. He develops a local explanation of the relationship between animist and Buddhist practices, one that does not generalize to other areas (see Durrenberger 1983).

It is the underlying axiom of power, its existence, and how one acquires it that accounts for many practices that are labelled "Buddhist." Anthropologists writing about Theravada Buddhism remark on the goal of every male spending some time as a novice or a monk, even if the reality does not match this ideal. The importance of power and the need for men to acquire power accounts for both the ideal of ordination and its frequency (Tannenbaum n.d.-b).

Two facts make this account appear Buddhist: first, tattoos and amulets draw on the power of the Buddhas and their teachings; and second, people acquire power through keeping Buddhist precepts. These actions only make sense in the context of the axiom of morally neutral power and how one acquires it. The quintessential element of Buddhism, the law of karma—the inevitable consequences of actions, both good and bad—with its moral implications is irrelevant to this discussion.

Merit-making through generosity is the most striking aspect of Theravada Buddhist ceremonies, yet it is unimportant in this account of power. Generosity is the means to validate and display one's power, rather than a means to acquire it. Powerful people stage merit-making ceremonies as evidence of their power and ability to organize the necessary resources. Through offerings to monks, they also assert their legitimate claim to power. Through these offerings, they accumulate merit that serves to legitimize and reinforce their present powerful positions. The ability to be generous is justified in terms of the law of karma.

Good and bad actions in this and previous lives determine a person's position in this life. Some people are rich and powerful because they have performed considerable good deeds in past lives and are now reaping the rewards of those actions. Others are poor because of misdeeds in previous lives, and their present position is a consequence of them. However, as Hanks (1962) points out, the actual balance of good and bad deeds is unknowable, and its assessment changes through time as the person's fortune waxes and wanes. Because karma is unknowable, people who make claims to legitimate power must validate them through public displays. Because its beneficial aspects can be depleted, people need to continually restock their store of merit. Public displays of generosity to monks serves both of these purposes.

Cosmology and Power in the Uplands and Lowlands

There are some striking continuities between the uplands and lowlands—primarily power and the central role it plays in determining how beings interact with one another. They share a similarly populated universe. In both uplands and lowlands, people conceptualize spirits in similar terms. Kirsch (1973: 12) citing Leach (1954) suggests that for uplanders, spirits are "magnificently non-natural men" and that "they extend the human class hierarchy to a higher level and are continuous with it." The essential difference between humans and spirits is visibility; spirits can always see people, but people cannot see spirits unless the spirits allow it. Some spirits are more powerful than humans, some less powerful. All beings are ranked in terms of relative power.

Buddhism adds a number of layers of heavens and hells to this basic cosmology, elaborating the rewards and punishments that actions in this world entail. For uplanders, life after death is unelaborated and is considered a continuation of life on this earth (Kirsch 1973: 16-17). There are no hells: good or bad, one goes to the same place. How one dies

74

rather than one's morality determines whether a person goes to the land of the dead or remains in this land. Lowlanders share the uplanders' horror of a bad or violent death, and both equally fear the haunting by the resultant spirit. In the lowland societies, dying a bad death is given a moral, karmic interpretation.

Uplanders and lowlanders share this basic conception of the universe. Nonetheless, how it is elaborated changes in the different political and economic settings. Power is subtly different in the uplands and lowlands, and the consequences of generosity differ. In both systems, power is an unelaborated basic assumption about the universe. Minimally, power and powerful beings exist. However, how one gains access to this power differs. For Shan, one gains power either through the practice of austerities or through the reliance on more powerful others. More powerful beings can provide direct protection, or one can draw on their power through amulets and tattoos. Powerful humans justify their power in terms of karma and legitimize their claims to it through generosity to their dependents, monasteries, and monks.

In the uplands, power is derived from wealth and proper conduct (see Durrenberger in this volume). Here, however, wealth is directly connected with productive capacity that is part of a person's fate given at birth. One's fate, or productive capacity, is only known through its realization as wealth and its proper usage. In egalitarian societies such as Lisu, honor/power is solely dependent on productivity. In hierarchic societies, a person may inherit a capacity to be productive. Nevertheless, in both situations, the unit making claims to productivity, be it a household or lineage, must demonstrate its productive capacity through sufficient wealth to host feasts and support its members in ways that validate its claims.

In the uplands, power/honor is not related to morality. Proper conduct is behaving as a human being and is better equated with knowing ones' customs and following them. Indeed, neither morality nor legitimacy are issues in the uplands. Honor, power, and productivity all mutually imply each other. If one were not honorable, and not able to live up to one's obligations, then one would not have power. Having power is an indication that it is legitimate—that one has honor and productivity.

In the uplands, power is linked to individual productive capacity, and actual production and wealth are evidence of that power rather than a means to it. A person may inherit a tendency to be productive, but the validation of that claim rests on the ability to produce. In the lowlands, power is not related to productive ability; rather it is linked to the control of productive resources. This difference is the difference between power/potency residing in the individual or group and power residing in the control of productive resources.

Throughout this area, people, households, and lineages gain prestige, power, and honor through wealth. In the uplands, it is the unit

75

producing the wealth that acquires prestige, power, and honor. In the lowlands, it is wealth, however acquired, which is both a cause and consequence of power.

States, Political Economy, and Ideology

When one moves from the uplands to the lowlands, one shifts from egalitarian or hierarchic to state political forms and from an economy based on swidden agriculture to irrigated rice. Ideology and world view are transformed in ways parallel to the changes in political and economic formations. Thus, one expects differences in ideology and world view between the upland and lowland groups to be related to these differences in political and economic forms.

In the uplands, power is, as Kirsch and Durrenberger argue, potency and fertility; it is given at birth, possessing it implies one is honorable, able to meet obligations, and has the respect of others. Evidence for possessing power comes from actual production and its display through feasting. In the lowlands, power is protection; people have access to it through being born into powerful families, protection from more powerful others, or the practice of austerities. Evidence for power comes from the ability to protect others and to behave without fear of the consequences. Unlike the uplands, legitimacy is a continual question, and power does not imply honor (see Table 1).

The lowland situation is complicated by the existence of different levels of society and the autonomous appearance of peasant communities. Ignoring for the moment the connection to a wider political economic system, lowland peasant communities appear remarkably similar to those in the uplands.

Consider the poor Shan village of Thongmakhsan, located in Maehongson Province. It consists of forty-one households, all dependent on agriculture for their livelihood except for two schoolteachers. They grow irrigated and hill rice for subsistence and sesame, soybeans, and garlic as cash crops. Approximately half the community makes both hill and irrigated fields, a quarter only irrigated fields, and a quarter only hill fields. Depending on the price of the cash crops most households also make a sesame garden and grow garlic and/or soybeans (Durrenberger 1977, 1981a; Tannenbaum 1982, 1984; Durrenberger and Tannenbaum 1983, in press).

TABLE 1

Upland and Lowland Power Compared

	Upland		Lowland
	Egalitarian	Ranked	
Power			
Nature	potency and fertility, honor		amoral power, protection
Source	fate; follow customs; live up to obligations	from lineage of birth; follow customs; live up to obligations	fate or karma; refuge in powerful others; restraint
Distribution	random	concentrated in lineages	random
Consequence	prestige and respect		freed from constraint
Evidence	productivity; ability to support household, lineages; sponsoring feasts		ability to protect others
Wealth			
Source	agricultural production; trade		villages: land agriculture states: taxes, tribute, corvée, control of people
Feasts			
Unit	household	lineage	household, community, states
Focus	analogous to feasting units		precept-keepers
Reciprocal	yes		precept-keepers: no lay audience: yes

Status within the community depends on households' ability to provision themselves, sponsor appropriate life-cycle ceremonies, and contribute to community-wide festivals. Agricultural production is the only source of wealth to support these activities. Currently, it is possible to legally own irrigated fields, while all hill fields are illegal and unownable. Sesame is a hill crop planted in swiddens. Soybeans and garlic are grown in drained irrigated fields after rice is harvested. Members of the community without these fields are given free access to those of friends or relatives.

Households with sufficient irrigated fields to provide all the rice they need are in a better position than those that rely on both kinds of fields or only hill fields. Irrigated fields are two or three times more productive per day's labor than hill fields, and there is less variation in harvest from one year to the next (Durrenberger and Tannenbaum, in press). They are in a position similar to those in a hierarchic community who control access to more productive land, but every household has access to some land. All households suffer from fluctuations in harvests, prices for cash crops, and from vagaries of weather, although those with irrigated fields are better protected from drought.

Only two households regularly produce rice beyond their subsistence and ceremonial needs. No household has sufficient land or labor to produce considerably in excess of its needs. Because there is free access to hill fields, no household has to rely on wage work for its livelihood. Households have to rely primarily on their own labor.

Like Lisu, these Shan strive to produce sufficient rice and cash crops to provision their household, sponsor ceremonies, and make contributions to village wide festivals on the same scale as everyone else. Respect and status are directly linked to agricultural production. No household has the resources to produce on a scale to dominate the others or can afford to sponsor large ceremonies on its own. Access to hill fields for rice and sesame production, free access to drained irrigated fields for cash crop production, and free access to the market produce a local economic context similar to that of the Lisu. One consequence is that within the community relationships are remarkably egalitarian, with prestige and status contingent on successful agricultural production.

This surface similarity masks underlying structural differences (see Table 1). One indication of this is in the variation in intensity of production in Thongmakhsan compared with Lisu. Lisu have a narrower range of intensity of production; consequences of over and under-production are both negative. Households that over-produce are seen as attempting to dominate others: Dessaint (1971) provides evidence where such attempts lead to assassinations. Under-production brings shame from the inability to meet obligations, diminished honor and power, and the loss of respect. For Shan, over and under-production do not have these connotations. For Thongmakhsan, the link between status and agricultural production is an artifact of its poverty; generally, status is linked with wealth and the control of resources rather than production, per se. Within Thongmakhsan, reaction to under-producing households varies: those that are having difficulty because of illness or other misfortunes are treated with respect, while others, either incompetent or lazy, receive little respect. Over-production is neutral; households intensify production to repay debts, develop irrigated fields, or build a new house. Lisu reject over-production because it implies someone trying to dominate the rest; they reject the principle of subordination. Shan do not. People in Thongmakhsan recognize that they are only poor villagers, ranking quite low on the scale of powerful beings: they recognize that they are subordinate to wealthy outsiders and government officials.

While public generosity and feasting are important in both the uplands and lowlands, the focus of the feasts indicates another structural dissimilarity. For upland societies, the unit sponsoring the ceremony and receiving the generosity are both part of the reciprocating system. In egalitarian situations, households sponsor feasts to which they invite other households, while in hierarchic communities high status groups offer feasts to other such groups. Participating in the feast implies at least temporary obligation and subordination to the feast givers. Obligations are partially repaid when the recipients give blessings, and are fully repaid when the recipient offers a similar feast and invites the original sponsor.

In lowland Buddhist settings, sponsors of feasts range from households to whole communities while the focus is always the same, precept-keepers. Precept-keepers are monks who keep 227, novices who keep ten, "nuns" (Shan, *mae* , "women"; *khao*, "white") who keep eight, and "old people" who daily keep five and keep eight on holy days during the rainy season retreat (Shan, *waa*; Thai, *phansa*). They are the focus of the feast because they have power and can give blessings (Tannenbaum n.d.-a). Monks, because they keep the most precepts, are the most powerful and can, therefore, give the most powerful blessings. Powerful beings do the donor the favor of receiving his offerings. Unlike the highlands where generosity always entails a claim to power and superiority, here generosity to monks entails the donor's admission of inferiority to the monks. Monks do not participate in prestige competition through reciprocal feasting; they stand outside and above the system.

While ceremonies are possible with only the presence of a sponsor and monks, this rarely occurs. Most ceremonies include other households in the community, people from outside the community, and a group of friends and relatives to help with festival preparations. Each group is important although they perform different functions. Precept-keepers, especially monks, receive offerings and a meal; they return blessings and merit to the sponsors and all people who attend. Guests are the public who witness the ceremony and are in a position to support the sponsor's claims. They are aware of the amounts offered, the number of monks invited, and the kinds and quality of foods served. Festival participants evaluate these relative to other similar festivals, and these evaluations are widely discussed. Participants admit temporary inferiority to the sponsors since they are recipients of food. Generally at a village level there is a sense of balanced reciprocity, guests expect to invite sponsors when they make similar ceremonies in the future. No festival is possible without helpers to prepare the foods and serve them. In a village, the people helping are likely to be friends and relatives, peers of the sponsors who expect similar help when they sponsor a celebration. In richer communities or where the sponsor is a powerful official, helpers are likely to come from the group of his dependents. Instead of the balanced reciprocity implied in villages, people who come to help are making statements of their obligation and dependency on the sponsor.[3]

Sponsors of ceremonies are making a number of claims about themselves and their relationships with followers, monks, and guests. The sponsor demonstrates his wealth by the size of the ceremony, quality of food, and number of monks. For wealthy and powerful individuals, the number of people who come to help also provide evidence of power. They also demonstrate their respect for and subordination to Buddhism. Since power is morally neutral and frees people from the consequences of their action, it is important for powerful people to publicly subordinate themselves to Buddhism. This subordination suggests that they will use their power properly and that it is a consequence of merit, although the source of their wealth and power is unknowable. The merit they make from their offerings should promote further legitimate wealth and success.

Buddhism is important in this system. The Buddha, his teachings, and followers are powers in their own right. The law of karma, the inevitable consequences of past actions where good deeds return good in this and other lives and bad deeds return misfortune, justifies and legitimizes the distribution of wealth and power. Monks, because they are powerful and stand outside and above the status competition, are a constant universal standard against which competitors can compare themselves. This position is not possible in the uplands where the foci of the feasts are also competitors within the system. There, all one can do is establish his position relative to others within the local setting. Because prestige and power are linked with personal productivity and because other competitors have similar access to the resources necessary to sponsor feasts, it is impossible to develop a monopoly of power or potency. The upland system is essentially open.

Kirsch recognizes the consequences of this difference in his discussion of the nature of the upland system. He states:

> no single unit can in fact monopolize the total "profit" of
> enhanced ritual status. This may of course occur in other
> systems. For example, the Shan theory of "divine

kingship" might be seen as such a system in which one position monopolizes ritual status. But in this hypothetical model of hill tribes society total monopoly of ritual status cannot occur because such status is measured only in relation to other similar units, and the economy cannot be completely "closed." ...Any tendencies to close this economy of ritual status through an absolute monopoly would involve a complete transformation of the economy and a shift to a new set of rules.... (1973: 7-8)

The upland ritual "economy," to use Kirsch's metaphor, is open; there is no limit to the number of players, nor to the amount of fertility or potency available. The audience for displays of wealth and the recipients of generosity are other players. The people who are the recipients of today's generosity are likely to be the sponsors of tomorrow's.

This is not the case in the lowlands. While the elite do not have a monopoly of power, either real and mystical, the gap between a poor villager and a powerful official is enormous. Villagers have some power, since all beings must, but the difference is so great that the elite might as well have a monopoly. Poor villagers know their lowly position in the system. They can see the difference in the quality of their lives and in the kinds of offerings they can make compared to those of officials and wealthy people. Offerings to monks provide a standard of comparison within the village; knowledge of the level of their offerings allows villagers to rank themselves vis-a-vis outsiders. Within the community everyone may strive to be recognized as a responsible member of the community, but the wealth and success this implies only puts them in the lower ranks of the total system. This type of information and knowledge serves to reinforce and justify the system of unequal access to resources.

The major difference between the upland and lowland systems is the different political and economic forms. The ideological consequence is the increased complexity and ambiguity in the lowland system. Access to power is through restraint and withdrawal *or* dependency on more powerful others, two radically different means with different consequences for behavior. Power frees people from the consequences of their actions and removes them from society and societal constraints. This contrasts with power in the uplands, which derives from production, and implies participation in society, not withdrawal from it. The consequences of gift-giving become ambiguous; they depend on the status of both the giver and receiver. Leach (1954) focuses on just this difference in his analysis of Kachin becoming Shan. Buddhism heightens this ambiguity and complexity. The law of karma legitimates the distribution of wealth and power and provides a moral element to power. This element is similar to, but not identical with, the upland notion of power deriving from proper behavior and establishes a surface similarity between the two systems. This superficial similarity is strengthened by the importance of publicly validating claims through feasting and generosity. Finally, the operation of the lowland system in areas where everyone is equally poor results in a similar egalitarian form within the community.

In the upland system, things are what they appear to be—power implies potency and the ability to meet obligations; there is only one possible interpretation. In the lowlands, the system, with its superficial similarities to the uplands, creates ambiguity and various plausible interpretations.

Acknowledgments

My research in Thongmakhsan during 1979-81 was supported by a grant from the Midwest University Consortium for International Activities and the International Fertilizer Development Center. My research in Mawk Tsam Pe during 1984-1985 was supported by a post-doctoral fellowship from the Social Science Research Council.

Notes

1. See Durrenberger (1977) for an account of villagers' obligations during the Shan period.

2. See Durrenberger (1980) for a description of one such ceremony.

3. See Errington (1983) for a discussion of this in Sulawesi.

References

Ames, M.
1966.   "Ritual Prestations and the Structure of the Sinhalese Pantheon." In *Anthropological Studies in Theravada Buddhism,* edited by M. Nash, 27-50. Southeast Asia Studies Cultural Report Series, no. 13. New Haven: Yale University Southeast Asia Studies.

Archimbault, C.
1959.   "The Sacrifice of the Buffalo at Vat Ph'u." In *The Kingdom of Laos,* edited by R. deBerval, 156-161. Saigon: France-Asie.

Blanchard, W.
1958.   *Thailand.* New Haven: Human Relations Area Files Press.

Boshe, J.
1971.   *Thailand: Land of the Free.* New York: Taplinger.

Condominas, G.
1975.   "Phiban Cults in Rural Laos." In *Change and Persistence in Thai Society,* edited by G. W. Skinner and A. T. Kirsch, 252-257. Ithaca: Cornell University Press.

deBerval, R.
1959.   "Profane and Religious Festivals." In *The Kingdom of Laos,* edited by R. deBerval, 126-127. Saigon: France-Asia.

Dessaint, A. Y.
1971.   "Lisu Migration in the Thai Highlands." *Ethnology* 10(3): 329-348.

Durrenberger, E. Paul
1977.   *A Socio-Economic Study of a Shan Village in Mae Hong Son Province.* Chiang Mai: Tribal Research Centre.

1980.   "Annual non-Buddhist Religious Observances among Mae Hong Son Shan." *Journal of the Siam Society* 68(2): 48-56.

1981a.   "The Economy of a Shan Village." *Ethnos* 46(1-2): 64-79.

1981b.   "The Southeast Asian Context of Theravada Buddhism." *Anthropology* 5: 45-62.

1983.   "Shan Rocket Festival and Non-Buddhist Aspects of Shan Religion." *Journal of the Siam Society* 71: 63-74.

Durrenberger, E. Paul and N. Tannenbaum
1983.   "A Diachronic Analysis of Shan Cropping Systems." *Ethnos* 48(3-4): 177-194.

in press. *Analytical Perspectives on Shan Agriculture and Village Economics.* Yale University Southeast Asia Monograph Series, no. 37. New Haven: Yale University.

Ebihara, M.
1966.   "Interrelations between Buddhism and Social Systems in Cambodian Peasant Culture." In *Anthropological Studies in Theravada Buddhism,* edited by M. Nash, 175-196. Southeast Asian Studies Cultural Report Series no. 13. New Haven: Yale University Southeast Asia Studies.

Errington, S.
1983.   "The Place of Regalia in Luwu." In *Centers, Symbols, and Hierarchies: Essays on the Classical States of Southeast Asia,* edited by Lorraine Gesick, 194-241. Yale University Southeast

Asia Monograph Series, no. 26. New Haven: Yale University Southeast Asia Studies.

Fried, M.
1967.   *The Evolution of Political Society.* New York: Random House.

Graham, A. W.
1912.   *Siam.* London: Alexander Moring, Ltd.

Hanks, L.
1957.   "The Cosmic View of Bang Chan Villagers, Central Thailand." *Proceedings of the Ninth Pacific Science Congress* 3: 107-113.

1962.   "Merit and Power in the Thai Social Order." *American Anthropologist* 64: 1247-1261.

Htin, Aung
1962.   *Folk Elements in Burmese Buddhism.* London: Oxford University Press.

Insor, J.
1963.   *Thailand: A Political, Social, and Economic Analysis.* New York: Praeger.

Kaufman, H. K.
1960.   *Bangkhuad.* Monographs of the Association for Asian Studies, 10. New York: Association for Asian Studies.

Keyes, C. F.
1977.   "Millennialism, Theravada Buddhism, and Thai Society." *Journal of Asian Studies* 36(2): 283-302.

1984.   "Mother or Mistress but Never a Monk." *American Ethnologist* 11(2): 223-241.

Kirsch, A. T.
1973.   *Feasting and Social Oscillation: Religion and Society in Upland Southeast Asia.* Cornell University Southeast Asia Program Data Paper, no. 92. Ithaca: Southeast Asia Program, Cornell University.

1975.   "Economy, Polity, and Religion." In *Change and Persistence in Thai Society,* edited by G. W. Skinner and A. T. Kirsch. Ithaca: Cornell University Press.

1977.   "Complexity in the Thai Religious System." *Journal of Asian Studies* 36(2): 241-266.

1982.   "Buddhism, Sex Roles, and the Thai Economy." In *Women in Southeast Asia*, edited by P. Van Esterik, 16-41. Center for Southeast Asian Studies Occasional Paper, no. 9. DeKalb: Center for Southeast Asian Studies, Northern Illinois University.

1985.   "Text and Context; Buddhist Sex Role/Culture of Gender Revisited." *American Ethnologist* 12(2): 302-320.

Klausner, W. J.
1972.   *Reflections in a Log Pond*. Bangkok: Suksit Siam.

Landon, K.
1949.   *Southeast Asia: Crossroads of Religion*. Chicago: University of Chicago Press.

Leach, E. R.
1954.   *Political Systems of Highland Burma*. Boston: Beacon Hill.

Lehman, F. K.
1963.   *The Structure of Chin Society*. Urbana: University of Illinois Press.

1972.   "Doctrine, Practice, and Belief in Theravada Buddhism." *Journal of Asian Studies* 31(2): 373-380.

Mangrai, Sao Saimong
1981.   *The Padaeng Chronicle and the Jengtung State Chronicle Translated*. Michigan Papers on South and Southeast Asia, no. 19. Ann Arbor: Center for South and Southeast Asian Studies, University of Michigan.

Maran, LaRaw
1967.   "Toward a Basis for Understanding the Minorities in Burma: The Kachin Example." In *Southeast Asian Tribes, Minorities, and Nations*, edited by P. Kunstadter, 125-146. Princeton: Princeton University Press.

Mendelson, M.
1961a.   "The King of the Weaving Mountain." *Journal of the Royal Central Asian Society* 48: 229-237.

1961b.   "A Messianic Buddhist Association in Upper Burma." *Bulletin of Oriental and African Studies* 34: 560-580.

Moerman, M.
1965.   "Ethnic Identification in a Complex Civilization." *American Anthropologist* 67(5): 1215-1230.

Nash, J.
1966. "Living with Nats." In *Anthropological Studies in Theravada Buddhism*, edited by M. Nash, 117-136. Southeast Asia Studies Cultural Report Series, no. 13. New Haven: Yale University Southeast Asia Studies.

Nash, M.
1966. "Ritual Cycle and Ceremonial Cycle in Upper Burma." In *Anthropological Studies in Theravada Buddhism*, edited by M. Nash, 97-116. Southeast Asia Studies Cultural Report Series, no. 13. New Haven: Yale University Southeast Asia Studies.

Obeyesekere, G.
1966. "The Buddhist Pantheon in Ceylon and its Extension." In *Anthropological Studies in Theravada Buddhism*, edited by M. Nash, 1-26. Southeast Asia Studies Cultural Report Series, no. 13. New Haven: Yale University Southeast Asia Studies.

Piker, S.
1968. "The Relationship of Belief Systems to Behavior in Rural Thai Society." *Asian Survey* 8(5): 384-399.

Rajavaramuni (Prayudh Payutto), Phra
1984. *Thai Buddhism in the Buddhist World.* Bangkok: Mahachulalongkorn Buddhist University.

Ramakomud, S.
1985. "Theravada Buddhist Values and Economic Development." *Crossroads* 2(2): 83-89.

Reynolds, F.
1977. "Civic Religion and National Community in Thailand." *Journal of Asian Studies* 36(2): 267-282.

Smith, B. (editor)
1966. *Religion and Legitimation of Power in Thailand, Laos, and Burma.* Chambersburg: ANIMA.

Spiro, M.
1966. "Buddhism and Economic Action in Burma." *American Anthropologist* 68: 1163-1173.

1967. *Burmese Supernaturalism.* Englewood Cliffs: Prentice-Hall.

1982. *Buddhism and Society.* Second edition. Berkeley: University of California Press.

Tambiah, S. J.
1970.   *Buddhism and Spirit Cults in North-east Thailand.* London: Cambridge University Press.

1976.   *World Conqueror and World Renouncer.* London: Cambridge University Press.

Tannenbaum, N.
1982.   "Agricultural Decision Making Among the Shan of Maehongson Province, Northwestern Thailand." Ph.D. Dissertation, University of Iowa.

1984.   "The Misuse of Chayanov; 'Chayanov's rule' and Empiricist Bias in Anthropology." *American Anthropologist* 86(4): 927-942.

1987.   "Tattoos: Invulnerability and Power in Shan Cosmology." *American Ethnologist* 14(4): 693-711.

n.d.-a.   "Shan Buddhism: Power, Protection, and Ethics." Unpublished manuscript.

n.d.-b.   "Power, Gender, and Buddhism: Gender in Thailand Reconsidered." Unpublished manuscript.

Terwiel, B. J.
1979.   *Monks and Magic.* Second Edition. Scandinavian Institute of Asian Studies, Monograph Series, no. 24. Copenhagen: Curzon Press.

Umavijani, M.
n.d.   "Thai Art and Literature in Relation to Buddhism." In *Buddhism in Thai Life.* Thai National Identity Board, Foreign Languages Publication.

Van Esterik, P.
1982a.   "Laywomen in Theravada Buddhism." In *Women in Southeast Asia,* edited by P. Van Esterik, 42-54. Center for Southeast Asian Studies Occasional Paper, no. 9. DeKalb: Center for Southeast Asian Studies, Northern Illinois University.

1982b.   "Interpreting a Cosmology: Guardian Spirits in Thai Buddhism." *Anthropos* 77(1-2): 1-15.

Virasai, B.
n.d.   "Buddhism in Cultural, Social and Economic Life." In *Buddhism in Thai Life.* Thai National Identity Board, Foreign Languages Publication.

Wells, K. E.

1975.   *Thai Buddhism: Its Rites and Activities*. Bangkok: Suriyaban
Publishers.

Wilson, C.

1985.   *The Burma-Thailand Frontier Over Sixteen Decades: Three
Descriptive Documents*.   Monographs in International Studies,
Southeast Asia Series, no. 70. Athens: Ohio University Center for
International Studies.

INTERNAL INFLATIONARY PRESSURES IN THE PRESTIGE ECONOMY OF THE FEAST OF MERIT COMPLEX: THE CHIN AND KACHIN CASES FROM UPPER BURMA

F. K. Lehman (Chit Hlaing)

The Chin peoples, who inhabit the mountains of westernmost Burma bordering India, and the Kachin (Jinghpaw), who live in Burma's northernmost mountain and adjacent regions of Yunnan and Assam (China and India, respectively), have been prominent in a good deal of anthropological discussion of such topics as asymmetrical alliance marriage systems, systematic oscillations between so-called autocratic and non-autocratic village political organization, and the importance, especially in upland South Eastern Asia, of the long-term interdependency between them and their civilized plains neighbors (the Burmese in the case of the Chin, the Shan, Burmese, Chinese and Ahom, in the case of the Kachins) for the general structure of their cultures and societies. A central consideration in all such discussions has been the association between their systems of differential social ranking and the institution of sacrificial feasting—called the feast of merit complex in that part of the world (see, for example, Fürer-Haimendorf 1953, Loeffler 1954, Stevenson 1943, Leach 1954, Lehman 1963).

I shall argue that the jural ambiguities of status/rank in these societies are a built-in source of inflationary pressures that can, when external economic conditions are appropriate, lead to substantial changes in the overall social-political order.

Consider the Central Chin (Lehman 1963). There were, and indeed are, three traditional ranks or general statuses: *bawi*, that is, aristocrats or lords, *chia*, or commoners, literally ritually imperfect, and *sal*, slaves. It is not necessary to go into all the ramifications of meaning of these classes, and in fact only the first two need be considered seriously here. I have described them all in the work cited above.

On the one hand, the *bawi/chia* distinction is deemed hereditary. There are a number of clans that are *bawi phun* ('clan'), and there are many more that are *chia phun*. Slaves are either those persons that have submitted themselves to this status for reasons of protection from enemies or captives taken in raiding and warfare. While I shall have next to nothing to say about slaves in this paper, it is worth mentioning at this juncture that this rank, like the other two, is full of ambiguity. The status is more or less hereditary; at least the children of female slaves are born slaves. But, of course, there can be no slave clans, and slaves are, however declassé, members of the clans of their respective owners. Now, the marriage price of any women is roughly a function of her rank or status, so that, in particular, the marriage price for a female slave may be substantially higher than that for many a female commoner, on the grounds that, after all, she is a member of a *bawi* clan (or—see below on the equivocal character of *bawi* rank—at any rate of a *bawi* lineage), and the marriage price for any such woman has got to reflect *phun thawh* (the value of the 'clan'—it is, otherwise a rate of compensation payable to a person by anyone found guilty of having defamed the accuser's ritual or social purity or rank).

Turn now to the *mi-chia* (*mi*, 'people'). Quite generally, such people try to deny that they belong to any clan on the grounds that clan is only important for aristocrats; but that excuse is insufficient for explaining this patently false claim of clanlessness. What is, in fact, at issue is that, on the one hand, commoners without practical hope, or ambition, of competing in matters of status rivalry claim, at least, to have no great stake in the matter, with, perhaps, the added consideration of wishing to minimize, symbolically, the significance of their lower standing. But, on the other hand, there are commoners, by clan at least, who have practical or effective ambitions in this rivalry, and, for them, of course, the thing is to discount the idea that status/rank (the *bawi/chia* clan distinction itself, ultimately) is rigidly hereditary. Thereby hangs my tale.

There is a legal principle that conflicts with the principle that rank is hereditary; it is the principle that rank may be won and lost through the conversion of economic-political success into ritual accomplishment, for example, through the feast-of-merit hierarchy.

This is no room to go into the considerable intricacies of this system of feasting, which I have described elsewhere (see also Bareigts 1980). But one must at least understand that rank, *bawi* rank in particular, requires to be validated by the giving, by the householder, of a graded series of rituals-cum-feasts. These feasts of merit, which most directly transform practical attainments into social and ritual standing, come in two interleaved series: feasts having to do with the activities of the house/household (chiefly having to do with the building of ever more elaborate and symbolically decorated houses and compound fences) and feasts having to do with a man's achievement in the wider world of hunting and warfare. And so, indeed, one of the requirements of building even a very modest independent house is the giving of at least small-scale feasts, and the occasional person without even these minimal resources may lose even *chia* standing and, in order to have a physical as well as social position in the community, be forced to seek the position of a slave to a householder of high aristocracy. He cannot validate his own standing; therefore, it must be derivative of that of his master.

In any case, this situation has got to mean that the only thing actually hereditary about rank is the right to try and maintain the position of one's father. Succession here is only presumptive not automatic (as usual, the Lintonian distinction between achieved and ascribed status simply does not work). Clearly, given the well-attested fragility of the general economy in this region of isolated and generally poor swidden-farming country, and the even more general vagaries of differential demographic success and of individual fortunes and abilities, there is a not inconsiderable likelihood that any given person born to a *bawi* household may not be able to maintain that position ritually. Moreover, given the fact that inheritance is, depending upon clan tradition, either by primogeniture or ultimogeniture, the chances are good that a non-inheriting son may fail to live up to his father's position. This condition is well understood in Chin folk sociology, and the figure of such a son, most saliently a non-inheriting son of a chief, as a *mi-hrawk hrolh,* a disillusioned, socially alienated, rather unreliable and devil-may-care sort of individual, is a common cliché.

Bawi rank then is definitely something that can be lost, but this potential loss is ambiguous; for, effectually, such a person is still of *bawi phun* (clan), though the lineage or lineage segment (lineage and segment are shown in Lehman [1963] to be a relative, not absolute distinction) descending from him is not of *bawi* standing. His *phun thawh* is certainly less than that of the true aristocrats in his clan, though it may, at least for a time, say a generation or so, continue better than that of the out and out commoner. If he or his descendants recoup their fortunes, then full *bawi* standing may readily be resumed in the usual way. If not, their claim to *bawi* clan standing becomes increasingly an embarrassment to all parties, and the result is undoubtedly that such a lineage comes to be held unreservedly a commoner *(chia)* lineage, and, once again, the question of its clan is allowed to rest in decent obscurity.

If rank can be lost, it can be gained, but this is not as straightforward an idea as it may seem; it is not simply a matter of illicit inference on the part of these people. Rather, it is the consequence of a sort of conspiracy between commoners, of one sort or another, who have acquired practical fortune and means, on the one hand, and aristocrats trying to reverse a decline—or trying to increase their *bawi* standing and political importance (for instance, by amassing an entourage of obligated clients), on the other hand. Let me examine this conspiracy a bit.

It takes resources to raise or maintain one's *bawi* standing, of course. Moreover, if one is to increase one's standing, there is no better way than to ensure that the marriage price for one's sisters and daughters is as high as can be got. In this matter, an interesting principle surfaces; whatever price one manages to extract from suitors becomes, by customary law, the 'traditional' marriage price for women of that whole particular lineage or segment.

Understandably, of course, there is pressure from others to restrict anyone's trying to raise such 'traditional' prices, as this sort of thing tends to throw the whole system of prices and of relative standings out of equilibrium and, furthermore, generally tends towards forcing costs upward towards the point where increasingly many people will be unable to meet them, thus endangering the system as a whole. The principle of trying thus to maintain system prices applies beyond the domain of the prestige economy in fact. For instance, consider the cost of hiring porters from village to village—a common expense in this mountainous region largely without roads. When official persons travel through the area, if they have enough money, they will try to attract enough carriers by offering higher than standardized rates, and this action is sufficiently resented so that the inhabitants of the region have attempted recurrently to get the government to enforce fixed maximum rates for this sort of service. But enforcement is at best lax, since many of the offenders are government servants. In any event, the complaint is that such an enlarged payment will, by local custom, at once become the standard rate, so that, sooner or later, local people needing carriers will be unable to afford hiring them—a genuine hardship.

It is, therefore, somewhat difficult to raise the asking price for one's women in marriage. In fact, other *bawi* of good standing will simply refuse to pay such prices initially, and this can threaten the asker's *bawi* standing, since that standing depends, in considerable measure, upon his ability to marry his women off to *bawi* of political and ritual and economic standing not better than his own. Wife-givers take precedence over wife-takers, and a good alliance marriage is a marriage in which one pays, so to speak, both for the ritual recognition of importance by those superior and for whatever political protection or potential economic assistance such wife-givers may afford the individual. Who then amongst *bawi* of generally good standing will pay inflated prices for women from lineages of no great standing, even if such lineages have recently acquired relative wealth? Not *bawi* of better standing or greater wealth, surely, and not even *bawi* of solid ritual standing but not such great resources, because they, too, can do better elsewhere!

However, we have already seen that there exist within the system lineages of quite doubtful *bawi* standing: either lineages within *bawi* clans trying to recoup their lost position, or lineages of out and out commoners 'on the make.' Such lineages, if they can marshall the resources, will always, within limits of course, be willing to 'pay extra' for the privilege of marrying a genuine *bawi* woman. The reason, again, is quite simple: a related jural principle inherent in asymmetrical alliance marriage systems generally. That is, that the standing of the issue of any given marriage is a partial function of the standing of the wife who bears them, just in case, of course, that it is a ritually full marriage, guaranteed by the payment of the highest price the wife's lineages can successfully ask—viz., its 'traditional' price for its own female issue of its own major wives. For, it is only a major wife, that is, one acquired at full price in the sense mentioned above, whose children can succeed to their father's ritual standing (or to a claim of such standing), and who may participate with her husband in his ritual performances in the feast of merit cycle—a participation that is essential in any such ritual.

So, in spite of all pressures to restrict such marriage price raising, de facto limitations upon this practice amount simply to the availability of someone somewhere in the community or region of commoners (one way or another) who is willing and able to meet any given asking price. Ordinarily, even the best *bawi* lineages will not try to raise resources by this means, for their need to maintain good relations with other 'good' *bawi* lineages will motivate them to submit to the general pressure against such a practice. But, when those of less exalted standing than they have put the prices up, they, too, in order to maintain their relative position, will have to do so, and hence an inflationary cycle cannot be avoided within the system as a whole.

Furthermore, let there be an infusion of wealth into the region as a whole from outside—say on account of new recourse to education or economic opportunities arising in the plains and valleys of Burma proper available to persons irrespective of their standing in the local society, and the inflationary cycle may be carried to almost any degree. In such circumstances, clearly, it is not surprising to learn that opinion favoring the abolition or evasion of the whole system of marriage prices (on the part of the poorer segment of the population increasingly unable to afford what are now traditional prices inflated at all ranks and levels) arises and grows. And in this connection, people try more and more to opt out of the attendant religious/ritual system that motivates the system of marriage payments, and to convert to foreign religions (Christianity in the north and center, Buddhism in the southern Chin hills). Even for the converts, however, whose motivations for conversion, of course, are far more varied and complicated than just the matter I have here attended to, general considerations of prestige and invidious distinction also work against such abolition. Nor is it surprising to learn that opinion is also marshalled towards at least restricting the scale of marriage prices—this by traditionalists and converts, both.

All the foregoing is not, however, the whole story; for not only the system of marriage prices but also the system of feasting itself become subject to these same inflationary pressures, and with much the same destructive results for this, too.

Consider now the fact that giving a feast requires that one be formally accepted as a feast-giver. True, an uncontrovertible *bawi* householder (supposing he has already given one or more of the feasts of lower grade prerequisite to the one he now offers) will easily be able (again, providing he can afford it all) to get the proposed feast accepted as such, since he will easily persuade others to attend as guests and witnesses. But remember the idea that giving, if it is to achieve merit, requires that the relevant public accept the act as such (Lehman, 1987).

Who, in this case, is the 'relevant' public? In the first place, they are the other *bawi* of the community and region who have given feasts of grade at least as high as the one now proposed. Secondly, perhaps more particularly, there are those particular *bawi* households that are one's matrimonial allies: one's *bawi* wife-givers and wife-takers. Without at least some of all these categories in formal attendance, the whole affair will fail and be held to be null and void. But even in the kind of case mentioned, the matter is not all that automatic; for, as is also the case on any formal ritual occasion, such as, say, a marriage ceremony, the persons who absolutely have to attend must be persuaded to do so by means of a formal set of categories of payment: the price for travelling, the price for crossing the compound threshold, the price (paid to a bride's mother) for having suckled her, for having carried her on the back in a blanket, and so on, seemingly without end. But, of course, in the case in hand, provided only that the feast-giver has maintained reasonably good relations with these other persons and households and lineages, these can be considered only ceremonial persuasions. And if some amongst any of the relevant categories refuse to come, it is all right as long as some others in each agree to attend.

What, now, of the aspiring commoner wanting to become *bawi*, as it were, by giving a series of these feasts? In the first place, obviously, he has got to get *bawi* marriage allies. We have already provided him with *bawi* wife-givers, of course, but his wife-takers, surely, are not yet of *bawi* rank. What *bawi* would pay a *bawi*-type of marriage price for a woman from such a lineage? Only, perhaps, a very declassé *bawi* intent upon riding his wife-giver's coat tails back into full *bawi* standing; or else yet another aspiring commoner persuaded he can do the same thing through such a marriage, namely, persuaded that his new wife-giver will succeed in the feast-giving game. For, if our man at issue does indeed succeed in becoming, however reluctantly and ambiguously accepted, a *bawi*-through-feasting, then, at law, his wife-takers, in case they have paid a full price for our man's daughter or sister in marriage, will be accepted at least in so far as their capacity to fulfill the requirement of attendance at his feast is concerned. In effect, then, it depends upon his *bawi* wife-givers and upon other *bawi* of equal or greater feasting rank.

Now, it ought to be plain that our aspiring feast-giver is going to have to pay a lot more to persuade these people to come to his feast than has hitherto been 'customary.' And so, we see the same inflationary cycle operating once more. For his new payments, providing he can find relevant people to accept the higher payments out of need or avarice or political advisability, will at once become the going rate. Furthermore, he will have to make the feast bigger, thus more expensive to give, in yet another way. For any given level of feast he will have to kill more animals, both sacrificial and merely gustatory, if he is to persuade the public to take the necessary interest; and while this is not a ritual consideration and does not set a formal and mandatory standard, it does make future feast-givers feel that they have to compare their efforts with the example he has now set in order to make themselves a name in the public eye as important feast-givers and important *bawi* generally.

When it is only the incredibly wealthy (or profligate and ambitious) man who can give feasts in these circumstances, the system of feast-giving and everything tightly connected with it in the general system of ritual ranking and associated native politics, begin to give ground, become rare, and go out of fashion. It may not disappear very quickly, but feasts become rare, plans for giving them get postponed longer and longer, because it takes longer to accumulate the wherewithal, and eventually postponed indefinitely. They are now given infrequently, often merely as a sort of nostalgic example for a public who either long for former entertainments and symbols of cultural identity or have never seen such a thing and are merely curious about ancient customs. The religious-cosmological meanings and values informing the system of feasts and so on tend to lose more and more in competition with new religions from outside that have more and wider political, economic, and general cultural saliency in more modern conditions. Inflation has, once again, blown the system up!

And yet, the old system, the old 'prestige economy,' to use Stevenson's (1943) felicitous term, may not be wholly dead in certain circumstances. Take away, or otherwise reduce, the effectual flow from outside that fuels this inflation, and the system, to a certain extent at least, comes back to life. Thus, during the period starting with the 1962 socialist revolution in Burma and extending more or less up to the present, the real value of the kyat (Burma's unit of currency) fell drastically. The official economy was able to import rather little in the way of the vast quantity of goods people needed or had got used to having that come from outside the country, including some basic commodities. Only the so-called black market was able to provide these things, through the smuggling trade, and this trade, based chiefly upon bartering in kind, made little use of the kyat. Its purchasing power thus reduced, the economic and exchange structure based upon it came to have far less superior attraction over the traditional local arrangements than had earlier been the case. It became, once again, of paramount importance to invest, so to speak, in one's fellow villagers and in the traditional organization of mutual dependencies and assistance, even for ordinary survival.

In a sort of Gresham's Law effect, the less inflated economy tended to drive out the more inflated, and it was of use to start again, on a very limited basis, however, investing one's labor and one's productive output in such things as feast giving, which, therefore, has witnessed a certain upswing in these latter years. But, so much for the Chin example. More exactly, regarding reference to Gresham's Law, it now becomes sensible to expend one's greatly devalued kyat in flavor of accumulating the 'currency' of greater (exchange) value, that is, the exchange counters and relations of the old, traditional prestige economy. Quite literally, the bad 'currency' drives out the good.

Let us turn our attention now, briefly, to the Kachin, so well-known on account of Leach's classic work on them (1954). But let us look at certain corrections that have been made to his facts and his analysis by the anthropologist LaRaw Maran (1967), himself a Kachin.

Leach discounts as mythic historicism the idea that the *gumlao* version of the traditional Kachin political order has, as Kachins universally insist, a fairly recent historical source. Maran has argued (see also Friedman 1979), however, that this source can be approximately pinpointed between the end of the 18th century and, roughly, the middle of the 19th century. Approximately, of course, because it was not a single event but a cumulative movement or development from assignable sources. I shall not recapitulate his historical evidence, but I shall make use of what he has to tell us. It is another example of a built-in inflationary source within the Kachin version of the feast-of-merit prestige economy being fueled from outside to the point where the system undergoes structural alterations.

The traditional Kachin (that is, Jinghpaw) political system involves hereditary chieftainship and the attendant stratification of clans into aristocratic and commoner sets. The heartland of this system is in the northwestern part of the Kachin territories. Here, we find the *gumchying gumtsa* chiefs, the classic 'thigh-eating' chiefs of the literature. In the areas where the valleys were more fully taken up by the Shans and their principalities (though the Jinghpaw even in their heartland had 'always' had some western Shan [and/or Ahom] principalities close by and had long been clients of these), an outlet had been found, for all one knows, deliberately sought, for the ambitions of the non-inheriting sons of chiefs. Here, in the new hill lands, they could carve out for themselves new domains as thigh-eating chiefs. This was, of course, supported by the bigger chiefs back home, so to say, not only because it gave them a safety valve for ever-simmering discontent, but also for another reason.

The home chiefs, in the *gumchying gumtsa* system, controlled access to the ritual underpinnings of chiefly status, because they controlled the hereditary priests or ritual officiants who are essential for the performance of the feast-of-merit-like ceremonies by which such a chief may, alone, achieve and raise his rank—therewith, also, the kinds of dues he may demand of the common folk and lesser aristocrats in his domain. For such an aspirant to achieve chiefly standing, he had to have the services of such a priest, and, effectually at least, he could get this service reliably only by applying to some greater chief, to whom, then, the aspirant became a client, and usually a wife-taker—for these, too, are a people practicing asymmetrical alliance marriage. This condition naturally meant for the superior chief-patron that he would get both a large addition to his wealth in the way of gifts, payments, and followers obliged to serve him in war and so on.

This is the system called *gumyu*, about which Leach has something to say but very incompletely and, perhaps, somewhat misleadingly. A man would set himself up somewhere as a chief, but to be recognized, and certainly to be raised to a ritually more serious chiefly standing, he had to submit himself to a patron. This notion of submission-cum-temporary renunciation of one's standing is the exact meaning of the verb *yu*, where the prefix *gum* indicates that the action is taken by someone with proper pretension or claim to aristocracy. It is important to keep this last observation in mind, since the same thing is true of the prefix on the expression *gumlao*, where the root to which it is prefixed, *lao*, means simply to rebel, revolt, or opt out. And so, it certainly cannot be the case that *gumlao* is, as Leach wishes us to suppose, an anti-aristocratic movement in principle, or an egalitarian one. But more of this later. The aspirant had to renounce his position, at least ritually, whilst asking the patron-chief to sponsor a series of rituals. The net consequence of this act would be the reinstallation and confirmation of the aspirant as a true chief of rank under the patronage of the sponsoring chief, who then backed the client's claims to standing with the power and prestige of his own.

It is true that some chiefs in what we may call the new lands did, for just the reasons Leach adduces, put themselves forward as similar to Shan princes. In doing so they put themselves into a rather different system of politics, for they were not dependent upon the system of installation under classical chiefs and priests from the older territories. These were the *gumtsa* chiefs, and it is incorrect, as Maran has shown, to confuse them with the *gumchying gumtsa* chiefs, hence to see Kachin chieftainship in general as a drift toward Shan models. In fact, as Leach properly observes, these *gumtsa* chiefs, proportionally to their degree of assimilation to the status of Shan princes, risked alienating themselves from their fellow Kachins as their necessary infrastructure of power, and this condition served as a limitation upon the expansion of the *gumtsa* system. Moreover, insofar as these *gumtsa* chiefs based themselves, like Shan princes, upon wet-land cultivation, giving up a base in swidden cultivation, they also deprived themselves of the services of Kachin priests, because these ritual services depended upon the maintenance by a chief of swidden lands. So much did this add to such a claimant's alienation from his Kachin colleagues that there seems to have arisen a sort of compromise system known as *gumrawng gumtsa*, which, being semi-Shan/semi-Kachin, was especially unstable. I shall say nothing further about this system, save to point out that indeed it did tend to be involved in some kind of oscillation with *gumlao*. But this again is not the same thing as a fundamental oscillatory relationship between something called chiefly rule and something called egalitarian rule.

But back to the main argument, and to *gumyu*. For reasons that Friedman (1979) in particular has explicated nicely, during the period mentioned, beginning in the late 18th century, the Kachin leaders in what I have called the new lands came into some rather new and relatively non-traditional sources of wealth. It had mainly to do with the fact that a major Chinese caravan-trade route passed right through the new lands, between the two ecological zones Leach calls Zones B and C, respectively, in such a way that the hill folk of Zone C, intermediate between A (which includes the *gumchying gumtsa* heartlands) and Zone B, the region of *gumtsa* concentration, looked down onto these routes and could both levy tribute from the caravans (and the Shan principalities that needed the caravan trade) and produce and sell products. Caravan traders were, in any case, seeking to expand into the region, notably for opium trade. The controversy between Leach and others (such as, Nugent 1982, 1983; Leach 1983) about whether or not the Kachins, in those long ago years, grew or traded in opium concerned chiefly the more traditional Zone A and its extension into the Singhpo area of Assam, and is irrelevant to the point in hand. As Leach argues (1954: 26 ff.), opium was grown (in fact extended under the impetus of the caravan trade) in Zone B (and C, to some extent) during this period, and the sporadic irrigated terrace cultivation of C is to be understood as, more than anything else, an indication that this zone was something of a military zone requiring patches of cultivation defensible under siege.

Anyhow, the consequence, from the present point of view, was that more and more aristocrats could amass both the wealth and the followers needed to think of attempting to attain chiefly rank. In turn, this had to mean that the competition for *gumyu* patronage went up significantly. Obviously, then, the costs of doing *gumyu* mounted considerably, too, and, at the same time, what we may conveniently call the 'waiting period' between the initial search for a patron and the final feast at which the latter 're-installed' the aspirant also became much longer than it had previously been when the ratio between aspirants and possible patrons was less. We also have to realize that, in rather the fashion I explained (1963) for the so-called 'democratic style' of rule at Tashon and Haka of the Chin area, the *nouveaux riches* here, though they were clearly of aristocratic birth and intent upon chiefly privileges (see my earlier remark about the aristocratic significance of the *gum* in *gumlao*), were, at least generally, trying to be 'chiefs' in quite a new way. It was now possible for more than one person in a given community to pursue a chiefly career, because wealth and a following no longer necessarily depended upon exclusive control of a definite and continuous tract of land. It could be based, instead, upon leadership in the trading-and-raiding game.

What seems in the end to have happened was that the waiting period became simply too long and the costs—which mounted, of course, proportionally to the period over which recurrent gifts had to be made—

intolerable. Moreover, the successful aspirant had somehow to become a traditional type tract-of-land chief in order to complete the *gumyu* process, and only very few, clearly, could even think of managing this. It also was not seen as particularly important in a region where one simply did not need a tract to control in order to attract a following. But without a proper domain, no aspirant could become a 'thigh-eating' chief, because the paying of dues in question, a hind quarter of each major animal killed in the hunt or at home, was motivated by the idea that the tract-chief owns these 'fruits of the land.'

Meanwhile, these Kachin, having come into more intimate contact than earlier on with the (Buddhist) Shan, came to learn something of Shan Buddhist ideas, amongst them the idea of *wipaka* (Pali for the 'fruits of merit or demerit' of one's actions) or *yupaka* (the bastardized Shan form from which Kachin borrowed the term—see Lehman 1977). Also, the question had arisen whether the game was any longer worth the cost, and debate seems to have raged over this issue. After all, the first stage in the process, which gives the whole process its name, *gumyu*, means to resign one's immediate claim-in-principle to true, thigh-eating chiefly privilege. The real question then became whether, having done this deed, which costs nothing, it was reasonable or necessary and proper, to try and get these privileges again and have them confirmed through a patronage that had less practical significance than before in the politics of the new economy.

Like most genuinely ethical debates, this one, of course, never managed to be resolved to everyone's ultimate satisfaction. One side, motivated surely in part by practical considerations of economy and immediate realities, argued, to some extent, if Maran is right, and basing their position upon Buddhist notions to the effect that everyone had equal right to try to obtain merit, that it made no sense to seek to have these paramount rights over others in the community. It is interesting, moreover, to observe that, when, later on, Kachins became subject to successful Christian missionary influence, Christian ideas of 'equality before God' and the like, were also called upon to justify permanent renunciation of chiefly privileges—privileges, not rank or responsibility for adjudicating disputes or, in general, preserving the jural order. These Kachin were the *gumlao*. Those persisting in the search for 'true' chiefdom remained *gumsa*, or, rather, *gumchying gumsa*, in principle.

It is, clearly, not astonishing that we find ever since that localities change from being the one to being the other. It all depends upon who can succeed by which means. As in all such ideological disputes, no party has unambiguous and unarguable right on its side. The *gumlao* position is, in terms of traditional Kachin ritual sanctions, at best chieftainship *manque*, whilst adhering to the other position is costly and risky, though the advantages from at long last succeeding may be very great—especially under a British colonial regime that prefers dealing with domain chiefs anyhow (as Leach points out). But the 'oscillation' that Leach (also Kirsch 1973) tries to assign causes to, between domain chieftainship *(gumsta)* and a system in which a community is ruled by a council of 'chiefs' *(gumlao)* is clearly a consideration—economic in the first place, ethical and inherently a matter of possibly unending debate in the local system of ideas, on the other. It cannot be thought of with nothing more to go on than a concept of internal structural limitations (as Leach would have it) or the notion of the ritual search for cosmic power (according to Kirsch). Rather, we have seen at work—certainly together with what both Leach and Kirsch have spoken of (the work of searching for practical power and for its ritually and cosmologically defined sources)—a major internally generated source of inflation (the *gumyu* system), which, fueled from without, once again creates an inflationary pressure eventuating in basic systemic change.

References

Bareigts, P. Andre
1980. *La maison Lautu et les fêtes de mérite.* Fengpin, Taiwan: By the Author.

Friedman, J.
1979. *System, Structure and Contradiction in the Evolution of Asiatic Social Formations.* Copenhagen: National Museum of Denmark.

Fürer-Haimendorf, C. von
1953 (1939). *The Naked Nagas.* Revised edition. London: Methuen.

Kirsch, A. T.
1973. *Feasting and Social Oscillation,* Cornell University Southeast Asia Program Data Paper, no. 92. Ithaca: Southeast Asia Program, Cornell University.

Leach, E. R.
1954. *Political Systems of Highland Burma.* London: Bell.

1983. "Imaginary Kachins." *Man* (N.S.) 18(1): 191-199; 18(4): 787-788.

Lehman, F. K.
1963. *The Structure of Chin Society.* Urbana: University of Illinois Press.

1977. "Kachin Social Categories and Methodological Sins." In *Language and Thought: Anthropological Issues.,* edited by W. McCormack and S. S. Wurm, 229-249. The Hague: Mouton.

1987.   "Burmese Religion."   In *The Encyclopedia of Religion,* vol. 2.
         Edited by M. Eliade. New York: Macmillan.

Loeffler, L. G.
1954.   "Zur sakrale Bedeutung des Buffels und Gajals fur Ahnenkult
         und soziale Feste in Gebiet Sudostasiens."   Unpublished
         Doctoral Dissertation, Johannes Gutenberg University, Mainz.

Maran, LaRaw
1967.   "Towards a Basis for Understanding the Minorities of Burma:
         The Kachin Example."   In *Southeast Asian Tribes, Minorities
         and Nations,* vol. 1, edited by Peter Kunstadter, 125-148.
         Princeton: Princeton University Press.

Nugent, D.
1982.   "Closed System and Contradiction: The Kachin in and out of
         History." *Man* (N.S.) 17(3): 508-527.

1983.   (Reply to Leach 1983) *Man* (N.S.) 18(1): 199-206.

Stevenson, H. N. C.
1943.   *Economics of the Central Chin Tribes.* Bombay: Times of India
         Press.

LISU RITUAL, ECONOMICS, AND IDEOLOGY

E. Paul Durrenberger

For all his attention to ecology, Leach (1954) does not make much of the opium trade in northern Burma or its consequences for the Kachin political systems he discusses (Maran 1967). Kirsch (1973) summarizes much information on ritual in the same area and shows that a pattern of oscillation between hierarchic and egalitarian forms is related to an ideology of potency as it works itself out in various local contexts. Lehman (1963) relates differences in Chin political organization directly to differences in their relations with lowland civilizations.

Lisu of northern Thailand are part of the same system. In Thailand today they are egalitarian but have been hierarchically organized in the past (Leach 1954: 51, 59). The same ideology of potency informs both hierarchic and egalitarian systems, as Kirsch has argued. Both forms are possible not because of the logic of this ideology or its internal dynamics, but because of differing economic conditions at different times and in different places. For Lisu, as others in the same system, whether the ideology of potency is related to hierarchic or egalitarian social and political forms depends on whether wealth is readily available to all through household productivity and trade or accessible only through indirect connections to the lowlands. Ritual is an important link as economic action takes ritual form.

Lisu are Tibeto-Burman people who live in the highlands of northern Thailand, southwestern China, and Burma (Dessaint 1971a). In Thailand, they live in autonomous villages scattered among those of other highlanders such as Akha, Lahu, Hmong, Yao, and Karen where they produce corn, rice, and opium in their swidden fields.

For Lisu, "religion," "ethics," "law," and "ritual" are not separate categories. All belong to an undifferentiated category called "*yî lî*," which might be best translated as "custom." Lisu engage in many kinds of interactions with culturally postulated super-human beings, as Spiro (1966) styles religion. Super-human beings, spirits, follow the same logic, constraints, restraints, and forms as visible earthly people, though they are not simple projections of social categories (Leach 1954: 182).

On any given day, some people of a Lisu village are likely to engage in such interaction in order to return a lost soul, to request a spirit that is biting a person to relent so that the person will recover from his malady, or to request a spirit to possess a shaman to provide information about what spirits are causing a misfortune. Such activity is significant in the social, political, and economic life of Lisu even though they do not differentiate it.

The information from a shaman enters into a diagnosis, which entails a complex process of reasoning about etiology aimed at fixing a cause. When people have examined various sorts of evidence and reached a conclusion about causality, they act on the analysis. Often they sacrifice chickens or pigs in order to rectify various misfortunes from failing crops to illness of the body (Durrenberger 1976a, 1976b, 1977a, 1977b, 1979a, 1980).

Lisu rituals follow a repetitive program. People prepare the altar(s) and offerings, hold a living animal and invoke the spirit, explain the offense to the spirit, offer the animal and other offerings to the spirit, ask the spirit to do what they want it to do (remove the disease, help find a soul, etc.), ask blessings of the spirit, offer the offerings again, apologize for the inadequacy of the prayer and ask the spirit not to be angry, and kill the animal and cook it. They then repeat the first eight steps above with "cooked" offerings replacing "live" offerings, eat the cooked meat, and then the participants tie threads on the neck or wrist of the beneficiary to convey their blessings to him or her.

Leach (1954: 12) rejects Durkheim's (1964) distinction between sacred and profane states or actions in favor of a distinction between pragmatic and non-pragmatic aspects of any action. The non-pragmatic component he calls ritual, without inquiring into whether an Englishman's notion of "pragmatic" ought be taken as universal. He argues that non-pragmatic components of actions communicate something from actors to their audience. Like Lisu, Kachin rarely eat meat that has not been ritually sacrificed. Whenever meat is distributed, one person makes the prayers, another butchers the animal, and so on. Leach argues that all of these acts communicate something about the performers. In doing ritual acts, individuals are claiming rights to certain prestigious positions. For Leach, "non-pragmatic" actions are meant to make political statements, and ritual is the language of such statements (Leach 1954: 13-16).

The fact that rituals are composed of repetitive elements, which combine in different ways to make the whole of the repertory of ritual, suggests an analogy with language and, hence, a communication function. But, one might wonder, as did Sperber (1974), why people would go to all of the pragmatic trouble to make such simple-minded statements to one another. The complexity of the "code" far outweighs the simplicity of its message.

The major empirical facts about Lisu rituals are that pigs die and people eat them. One household among those of a village kills one or several of its pigs, each a form of wealth and an embodiment of labor, and furnishes distilled liquor to drink and sour bamboo shoots to eat with the pork and rice. Visitors from the same and other villages eat and drink together.

If there are messages in these rituals, they are that someone is suffering a misfortune for some cause, an act for which he or she is responsible, which entails either an offense to a spirit or the soul's wandering away because it does not want to stay among the living. If there is an offense, it is against a powerful being, which indicates that power exists and can be used to punish offenses against powerful beings, just as among ordinary humans, each of whom is powerful. A victim tries to rectify the offense and set the situation right by offering wealth to the spirit in order to repair the breach and restore its diminished power. If the spirit accepts the offerings, it is obliged to relent. Spirits and people confer blessings on one when they are thankful, when they have gratitude towards one. Giving food to the spirit evokes its thanks, and hence its blessings. The same is true of people. The ritual, then, "says," "I give food to people and spirits, they are thankful, and give me blessings, which augment my wealth, which I use to feed people and fulfill expectations and gain power." The rituals affirm that power exists, that one gives wealth to others, they return thanks, which gives one blessings, which gains one more wealth.

The rituals do not really "say" these things. Lisu are clever enough to think of less cumbersome ways to say things and parsimonious enough to think it foolish to expend such wealth on such a banal message. Rather, the rituals are a pragmatic way of dealing with the reality of misfortune, a mechanistic response to a mechanistic universe.

While the immediate "reason" for most ritual is to rectify a misfortune, illness of the body or of some other kind, any person's position in a Lisu village, any person's worth as he or others assess it, depends on the willingness and ability of his household to sponsor such feasts. When we examine Lisu ritual we see more than an expression of ideology, an enactment of world view assumptions. In addition, we see egalitarian people remaining equal, gaining honor, and building power. The mechanisms of dealing with misfortune, of power, of social manipulation, are consequences of a particular representation of reality, a particular set of axioms about reality, a world view. The fact that they are used to uphold egalitarian social relations is a consequence of the economic circumstances of the people. In other economic contexts, similar ritual based on the same world view validates hierarchic social relations.

Lisu are not alone in their world view or ritual. Here I describe relations among Lisu ideology, ritual, economics, and politics. I then show that the same ideology underlies the actions of other highlanders and suggest that it extends into the lowlands where it informs state systems.

Ideology

Lisu live in a world of beings of differential power *(dù)*, only some of whom are visible as people. Those that are not visible, spirits *(nì)*, have the same characteristics as human beings, but more or less power. As their part of contractual relationships with people, some of these, such as lineage spirits and the village guardian spirit, take care of people and keep them from harm. People make annual offerings to these spirits to renew the contractual relationships.

Power is derived from proper comportment and generosity. Generosity rests on wealth. Therefore, there are two components to power: wealth and proper conduct. People and spirits accrue power in the same way: by the production of wealth, by carrying out their contractual responsibilities, and by meeting the expectations of others, that is, being honorable. People produce wealth by working in their fields. Spirits get wealth from the offerings of their descendants. "Honor" and "power" are the same. The longer a spirit is in the land of the dead, the more offerings it receives from its descendants, the more often it has helped them, and the more powerful it becomes.

Spirits that have been in the land of the dead for only a comparatively short time, those of one's parents and grandparents, are relatively powerless. They cannot ride a shaman. One's great-grandfather is the most junior of the lineage spirits that can ride a shaman and provide any useful information or help in the realm of the spirits. Those who have died 'bad' deaths, involving drowning or bloodshed, do not go to the land of the dead, receive no offerings, stay on the face of the earth, and are less powerful than people.

While some spirits help and protect people in contractual relationships, any powerful spirit can be offended and hurt people. Like people in this egalitarian society, their recourse is negotiation and self-help if that fails. Since people cannot see spirits, and do not know what is offensive to them, they do not initiate apologies when they have offended spirits. Spirits then have recourse to self-help and do some damage to the person, his household members, his livestock, or his crops. The spirit causes some misfortune. To remedy the misfortune, if causality is not simply mechanical, due to natural causes, the person must ascertain which spirit is responsible, what the offense was, what the spirit would accept as settlement, and make restitution. A shaman can invite his great-grandfather spirit to ride him as an entrée into the spirit world to discover these facts, and the victim or his friends or relatives can then act on the information to remedy the misfortune.

The quality of one's fate *(myī)* is evidenced in one's palm line, if one could read it. When one is born, the high god, Wusa, assigns a limited life span. When it is finished, and one dies, one's "fate has arrived, been used up." Fate is qualitative—it can be good, bad, or indifferent. It is a measure of one's innate abilities and invulnerabilities. There is no a priori way to discover what a person's fate holds for him. It is an innate characteristic, the quality of which can be discovered only by the course of events in life.

"Honor/power" *(dù)* is related to the concept of "fate." The converse of power is "shame" *(sá tuá)*. Shame results in a loss of honor. Power is the ability to honor one's claims and others' legitimate expectations. If a person cannot offer hospitality to visitors, does not meet contractual obligations, wears shoddy clothing, or asks for loans, then he has shame.

When spirits speak to people through possessed shamans (see Durrenberger 1976a), they often say, "I have come to look for honor." Lineage spirits should help cure people, and if they do, they meet the peoples' expectations of them and gain honor. People remind the spirits of this in phrases such as: "Before you died, you had honor, do not lose it now." In one protracted illness, one of the shaman's lineage spirits addressed another, "You always stay in the house, but you do not take care of our descendants, so they have become sick and I am ashamed. Descendants of other spirits do not get sick," and "Other spirits came and made a ceremony, and I am ashamed." Even spirits, if they do not do what people can legitimately expect them to do, can lose honor and be shamed (Durrenberger 1976b).

Wealth is central for a person's being able to meet the demands and expectations of others—to be able to offer hospitality, pay fines of household members should they be necessary (see Durrenberger 1976c), or to provide bride price for sons. Wealth *(fwù chî)* is the tangible manifestation of intangible blessings *(ghà swî)*. Lisu often appeal to spirits to give them blessings in phrases such as, "If this person does not have blessings, please put blessings," "Put the blessings of silver, the blessings of gold." When lineage spirits possess shamans, they sometimes say, "The people tell me they do not have blessings, so someone has become sick." People can also give others blessings as indicated in prayers, "Let the people put blessings." When a child is sickly, the parents may seek a ritual foster parent for him. The foster parent transfers some of his blessings to the child by tying a string on around his neck. On other occasions people may give blessings by tying strings on others.

When a person makes a ceremony, he generally gives offerings to spirits, so that they will speak well of the person and give him a blessing. When one kills a pig for guests to eat or builds a rest house, bridge, or path side bench for public use as part of such a ceremony, a wider public benefits. When people eat at a feast following a ceremony, they give their direct blessings by tying strings onto the beneficiary. When people use a structure, they are thought to think or say something to the effect that the person who constructed it is a good person and thereby bless him. Good speech results in blessings and is the result of offerings given to spirits and the food and structures given to people.

If one has wealth, he can give things to people and spirits and cause them to speak well and give blessings. The fulfillment or manifestation of blessings is wealth; and so, the more wealth one has, the more one can hope to gain by feasting.

Favorable speech is a result of the speaker's general obligation *(chì yî)* to the person who benefited him. This practice is on the order of generosity, a feeling that one ought to do something for someone who has benefited him. If the recipient of a favor does not return it, it is said that he feels no *chì yî*, no generosity or obligation. It can also be said that he simply does not know the customs of the people. When people eat at a ceremonial feast or use public structures, they are presumed to feel generously disposed to their benefactor and give blessings in return either by tying a thread or good speech.

If someone has wealth, he can give things to people and spirits who feel generously disposed toward that person, speak well of him, and give blessings, the fulfillment of which is wealth. If a person does not feel generous in situations where he should, he loses honor and is shamed. If one has wealth, he cannot only feel generous but be generous and fulfill general expectations having to do with dispensing wealth, thereby gaining honor. Finally, one's fate is only known by his wealth.

Since inheritance is limited to ornamental jewelry that is not alienable, wealth must be the result of an individual's own productive efforts in a household production unit. Households are the units of production, consumption, honor, power, and self-help (Durrenberger 1976c, 1976e). When someone in a household has offended a spirit, the spirit may attack any member of the household.

Everyone has equal opportunity to work the same lands; all have access to the same technology. Thus, wealth is directly related to household productivity. Honor is a direct consequence of wealth because one can fulfill general and specific expectations only to the extent of one's resources. Wealth is a consequence of productivity. One cannot infer a person's or household's honor/power from position, lineage, filiation, name, or any other such indicator except wealth, which is a result of household productivity.

Spirits have honor—based on productivity—in the same sense people do. It follows that spirits represent some capacity or potential for productivity. There are spirits for each ecological domain recognized and used by Lisu: jungles, fields, streams, etc.; there are spirits for the criteria used for evaluating agricultural fields: amount of sunlight, tree growth, soil type; and there are spirits for political divisions into which lowland kingdoms have been organized: kingdom, province, county, township, village. The ecological areas are productive and used by Lisu; the criteria for good fields are agents of productivity. The political domains, although they are not an aspect of Lisu life, are known to be productive in terms of taxes and perquisites. There are many spirits that represent things that enter production or are productive in some way (Durrenberger 1980). Just as productivity is a measure of human potency and honor, it is a general measure of potency. For non-human objects, it is mapped onto a set of spirits (Durrenberger 1982).

There are other spirits such as hungry ghosts of bad deaths and the spirit of malicious gossip with less power than people. They cannot be offended or receive piacular offerings, though they may cause misfortune. Powerful and offendable spirits are beings posited by the mapping of the notion of productivity onto some occult entity. It follows that all productive things have some occult mapping (Durrenberger 1980).

Since humans are productive, they should have an unseen, occult component, a soul. Lisu hold that when a person's soul is absent he exhibits symptoms of malaise and does not go about the business of production. This connection is made quite explicitly, and it is said that if one loses his soul, he loses blessings, cannot work, and loses wealth and potency. Therefore, when the soul is absent, a person loses his productive capacity. The idea that people have souls is itself an implication of this more general logic according to which there is a mapping from productive entities to occult ones (Durrenberger 1975a,b,c,d, 1980).

The basic assumptions are: power flows from wealth; wealth is the result of productivity; power can be lost; and power can be reinstated by presentations of wealth. These beliefs underlie the logic of offense, retribution, and apology for people and spirits alike (Durrenberger 1980).

Economic Correlates and Contexts

Lisu produce three main crops in highland swiddens: rice, opium poppies, and corn. They eat the rice, sell the opium or exchange it for labor, and feed the corn to their pigs (Durrenberger 1974, 1976c, 1979b). Rice production returns more to labor than opium production (23.26 baht per day versus 9.45 baht per day [1 baht = US $.05]), and so people prefer to produce their own rice if possible. If the fertility of nearby fields (within a day's walk) has declined to such an extent that rice production is not feasible, they will purchase rice with the proceeds of their opium cultivation. The lower the productivity of nearby swiddens for rice, the more they rely on cash crops to purchase subsistence goods (Durrenberger 1979b).

The largest use for the value people produce is for subsistence (46%); the second-largest use is for consumer goods (28%); the third-largest use is for reciprocal exchanges (18%: 14% for feasts and 4% for other reciprocal exchanges); and the smallest is for investment in further production (8%) (Durrenberger 1976c).

Sponsoring feasts is a means of showing that one is an honorable person, someone who can meet his obligations, including reciprocating feasts that members of his household have attended in the past. The number of pigs a household keeps is a readily observable measure of its ability to meet such obligations. Other readily visible measures of a household's ability to reciprocate feasts and meet other obligations are attire and household furnishings. These are general measures of wealth, or potency in Kirsch's terms (1973).

Households keep a mean of 14.4 pigs, mainly for sponsoring feasts. Most of the value expended in reciprocity is in the form of feasts and accounts for 14% of total value produced. Expenditures for reciprocity and consumption are highly correlated at .94 (all correlations cited are Pearson's). The number of pigs a household has correlates .59 with reciprocity expenditures and .63 with consumption expenditures (Durrenberger 1976c).

These correlations are consistent with the idea that the number of pigs a household keeps is an observable measure of its ability to meet its obligations. Other such measures are the attire and household furnishings of a household, both general measures of wealth or potency (Durrenberger 1976d, 1986).

One source of wealth for Lisu is opium production. Seidenfaden, writing of the first quarter of the 20th century, says that Lisu grew opium poppies but were not "much addicted to the smoking of opium" (1967: 118). Bernatzik (1970), whose observations were made in 1936-37, argues that because the Thai government had agreed to purchase opium from British India and not produce it, it was expensive to purchase, and so a contraband trade developed in the hills. This demand caused production to increase.

> The business proved to be so lucrative [to Chinese traders] that they persuaded the inhabitants of whole villages, especially the Lisu, but sometimes also the Akha...to apply themselves exclusively to the cultivation of poppies and to exchange opium for food supplies from their neighbors. (Bernatzik 1970: 697-98)

There is still a ready market for opium. Opium traders come to highland villages to make purchases and pay in cash (see McCoy 1973).

Mainly because of the opium trade and nearby Thai markets, wealth is available to all Lisu households equally. All can participate equally and gain recognition as honorable in terms of the ideology of honor that, in these circumstances, recognizes only productivity (Durrenberger 1974, 1976d).

Most Lisu villages are not more than a day or two's walk from a lowland Thai town with a market, and so there is access to markets as well as money to purchase cloth, kerosene, thread, needles, lamps, soap, medicines and other items (Durrenberger 1974, 1976d).

Sahlins (1972) argues that general reciprocity, giving wealth with no expectation of specific return, may lead to hierarchic political forms. Since some households have lower consumer/worker ratios, they can provide more general reciprocity than those with high consumer/worker ratios. This is the germ of a redistributive system. For highland hierarchic systems, Kirsch (1973: 7) argues that success in status competition is related to the economic success of households and suggests (Kirsch 1973: 30) that this might be related to household composition. Leach's discussion of hierarchic Kachin forms (1954: 163-4) and Lehman's of hierarchic Chin forms (1963: 144) suggest the type of relationship Sahlins discusses.

The larger the consumer/worker ratio, the more work it takes to provision the household and the less labor is available for any other sphere. Thus, there should be a negative correlation between consumer/worker ratio and expenditures for reciprocity (but see Tannenbaum 1984 for a discussion of testing hypotheses on the basis of consumer/worker ratios alone). This is not true for Lisu. Households with low consumer/worker ratios and more available labor should produce more and engage in more reciprocity. There is a low but positive correlation (.14) between the consumer/worker ratio and the value of pigs sacrificed (Durrenberger 1976c).

Each household desires to engage in the reciprocity to the same extent as all others, regardless of the availability of labor from the household as determined by the consumer/worker ratio. Since the ability to engage in reciprocity is gauged by consumer goods, each household also purchases consumer goods without reference to its consumer/worker ratio. The households with high consumer/worker ratios can only do this by incrementing their own labor by hiring labor from outside the village (Durrenberger 1976d).

Some households give more feasts and more lavish ones than others; some households are more successful than others. But this does not lead less successful households to join with more successful ones to form larger units of production, consumption, and feast sponsoring.

Less successful households remain independent, and their members express no desire to join others. There is always the chance that one's fate has not manifested itself, that one's bad luck will change, that better decisions and more astute agricultural judgments will lead to better harvests, and that hard work will eventually pay off.

If there were no such hopes, then less successful households might join more successful ones to start forming the larger social units Kirsch discusses. This might be the case in a situation of limited wealth and markets. In fact, Lisu production is geared to those households with the highest consumer/worker ratios, those in the worst production positions are taken as the norm against which others gauge their production efforts (Durrenberger 1984).

Households with the worst production possibilities cannot only expand their labor by hiring labor; they also provide the ceiling for all production. The urgency of production diminishes as the source of demand diminishes. This ratio is in contrast to lowland Shan, where the urgency of demand remains constant whatever the source of demand. Thus Lisu underproduce. Households with low consumer/worker ratios work less than they could. Shan overproduce, and households with low consumer/worker ratios work more than Lisu consider reasonable (Durrenberger and Tannenbaum, in press).

Economic conditions external to the village play a large part in determining how the ideology of honor, which informs feasting, is realized in social organization and action. Because of the regional context of the economies of Lisu villages (see Durrenberger 1974), there are sources of wage labor to hire to even out differences in consumer/worker ratios, a market for opium that provides money income, and sources of consumer goods on which to spend the money.

Egalitarian and Hierarchic Forms

Kirsch (1973) identifies hierarchic and non-hierarchic forms of organization in highland Southeast Asia. Lisu in Thailand have all the hallmarks of egalitarian organization. Each village is independent of the others (Dessaint 1971b). There are no headmen who make decisions for villagers, and Lisu loath assertive and autocratic headmen (Dessaint 1971b: 337).

Patrilineal lineages are not ranked, and lineage connections are not important for political alliances. Allegiance groups, which tend to cluster around groups of sisters and form on the basis of interests, are more important than lineages (Dessaint 1971b: 341-342). Members of each lineage follow lineage ritual customs, and some households have idiosyncratic ritual customs. There are no developed lineage mythologies, nor are there competing mythologies of foundations of villages. Lisu are very disinterested in origin stories of any type.

Land is held in usufruct, and members of each household stake out swiddens independently. No one claims to own any land. Since land is not owned, it is not heritable. The only wealth items that are heritable are silver ornaments that are inherited equally. Women's ornaments are passed on to daughters, while men's ornaments go to sons. Each household tries to provide a brideprice for each of its sons.

There is no set of overtly ranked feasts, although soul-calling and other curing ceremonies are often occasions for feasts. This catalog of characteristics indicates that these Lisu are egalitarian in contrast to others who are hierarchic (see Kirsch 1973).

Some Lisu may have been organized hierarchically in the past. Forrest (1908: 261) reported that some Lisu in southwestern China were under the nominal control of Chinese chiefs, some had their own headmen and did not recognize any authority, and some villages had no Chinese or other chiefs or headmen. Rose and Brown (1911: 264) said that Lisu on the Upper Salween had their own hereditary chiefs who ruled several nearby villages and that some isolated villages recognized no chiefs. Writing of Lisu of the Fang area of northern Thailand during the first part of the 20th century, Seidenfaden (1967: 118) said they were "governed by hereditary chiefs." Goullart (1955) reports that Black Lisu were among a group of small local "states" that paid tribute to the Dalai Lama in Tibet in a "feudal" system.

Although this evidence is spotty and inconclusive, it is enough to suggest that some Lisu have been hierarchically organized. This form of organization may have been to facilitate relations with lowlanders such as Shan and Chinese who may have seen to it that there were "chiefs" with whom they could deal in the same way as Thai officials nowadays appoint village "headmen." On the other hand, it may have been the result of the dynamic of alternating hierarchic and non-hierarchic systems described by Leach (1954), Lehman (1963, 1967), and Kirsch (1973).

To account for the oscillation between hierarchic and egalitarian forms, Kirsch de-emphasizes external relationships in favor of internal processes. He argues that people try to maximize a quality of "fertility" by sponsoring feasts that demonstrate "the sponsor has certain *innate qualities* of 'potency' which qualify him for...'prestige'" (1973: 18). Less successful households try to establish relationships with more successful ones that become larger units. A few large units develop and compete directly with each other. This decreases stability, and so alliances among these groups become important. Since group achievements are more important than individual ones, people try to associate with groups that have attained high ritual status. Since wife-givers are superior to wife-takers, any unit that gives wives to another must persuade the other to recognize it as superior. None of the major competing groups is willing to admit inferiority, so they must give wives to less successful groups. While wife-givers want to fix the relationship, and thus their superior status, wife-takers want the relationship to be flexible so they can ascend in the prestige competition.

As groups achieve higher rank, more people want to marry their women, but members of high prestige groups do not want to marry women of other groups because this would be an admission of inferiority. Men of high-ranking units, therefore, get wives from valley-dwelling Shan. Then the chief of the group becomes analogous to a Shan prince and cuts his relatives off from status achievement. For the chief's kinsmen who want to achieve prestige, this shift justifies a "revolt," an establishment of egalitarian relationships, and there is a return to a situation in which each household competes with each other household.

Echoing Steward's cultural ecology, Lehman (1963) attempts to explain differences between hierarchic northern Chin and non-hierarchic southern Chin partly in terms of differences in availability of secure trading opportunities and wealth with which to trade (also see Maran 1967).

Though Leach (1954) discusses "ecology," Maran (1967: 138-139) points out that he neglects the most significant relationship, that is, that egalitarian *gumlao* forms are associated with opium production while the hierarchic *gumtsa* forms are not. The hierarchic forms are three rather than Leach's one: a highland form with active chieftains and little connection to the lowlands; a lowland form of feudatory chiefdoms similar to Shan; and a disorganized form with powerless figurehead chieftains. The disorganized form, he argues, can develop into one of the others.

Where there are possibilities of trade and accruing wealth, there are egalitarian political forms based on reciprocal exchanges. Where there is no means by which everyone can accrue surpluses to use for social goals such as enhancing prestige, there are hierarchic social and political forms (Durrenberger 1976c).

In order to gauge another's innate qualities, one must examine the exterior indicator of wealth. In a hierarchic situation there would be a scarcity of lowland goods; money and markets would be remote. This situation is suggested in the early reports of hierarchic Lisu from Rose and Brown (1911) and Forrest (1908). If there is a hierarchic form of organization, some person must be able to claim superiority, and others must recognize his claim. Goods would be distributed by means of exchanges among lineages and by heredity as Lehman (1963) describes for Northern Chin. Why should material possessions obtained in these ways give one claim to influence or superiority? Because the possession of them implies superior innate characteristics. Wealth implies honor, power, and the superior quality of one's fate following the logic outlined above. Just as a person's honor is attributed to his productivity in an egalitarian situation, in a hierarchic one, his honor would be attributed to the source of his goods, his position in the round of exchange and heredity. The qualitative aspects of a person's fate can be predicted if the source of his wealth is known. If the source of wealth is the wealth of his parents, then it follows that innate qualities are heritable. Of course, individuals who inherit rank must validate it in practice.

These concepts involved in the ideology of honor are central to the operation of social relations in both the hierarchic and egalitarian conditions, but with rather different consequences for action. In the hierarchic situations they allow one to assume that someone has better fate, more honor/power/potency than oneself on the basis of given information such as parentage. In the egalitarian situation, one must prove constantly that one has as much honor as anyone else. Thus, one would expect something of a work ethic and consumerism among non-hierarchic systems as Kirsch (1973) suggests. The ideology of honor, the elements of the world view that concern qualities of people and their implications, are the same in either case since wealth implies honor regardless of the origin of the wealth.

In highland Southeast Asia, there is an ideology of honor and wealth that can be translated into rank and prestige under certain circumstances. Where wealth and access to valued goods are scarce, hierarchic forms will develop; where they are widespread, egalitarian forms will develop. Both hierarchic and egalitarian forms are based on the same ideology, but the social forms are largely shaped by economic relationships.

This ideology would allow for the development of political systems similar to those described for Northern Chin or highland hierarchic Kachin if there were few opportunities to acquire goods or money. If, however, the people live in a situation in which there is relatively easy access to both goods and money, the non-hierarchic variant would result.

If we interpret the historical evidence as suggesting that some Lisu have been hierarchically organized, and accept the assumption that this was not due to direct political manipulations by neighboring people, then we must take account of both the ideology of honor and innate qualities (as Kirsch has argued) and the economic conditions exterior to villages (as Lehman has argued), but neither of these is sufficient.

We see that to understand the Lisu in terms of the oscillation, or possibility, of hierarchic and egalitarian social forms, which the historical evidence suggests is reasonable, we must account for both an ideology of potency and esteem and economic conditions exterior to particular villages. Furthermore, the logic of potency is not confined to judgments about people but has a central place in Lisu cosmology (Durrenberger 1980, 1982).

Conclusions

Lisu gain prestige to the extent that they distribute wealth to others in reciprocal feasts. At the same time they are egalitarian and resent efforts at domination or control (Durrenberger 1976e). To sponsor feasts as events to gain prestige would leave the sponsor open to the charge of domination. At best, fellow villagers might move away, leaving one with a few supporters in a small village. At worst, they might assassinate the domineering person (Dessaint 1971b). To sponsor a feast as a remedy for a misfortune or therapy for a disease could carry no such implication. There is often a range of ceremonies for the same purpose. One may make a small or large ceremony. If one wants to advance prestige, he can choose one of the more lavish rituals.

Rituals distribute wealth and enhance the prestige of the sponsor without opening him to the charge of ostentation or presumption. The rhetoric of feast sponsorship is therapeutic, and the consequences are economic and social, involving enhancement of prestige (Durrenberger 1979a).

For Lisu, fate is unknowable. Spirits are mappings of productivity onto occult beings. Productivity is power. Wealth gives one the where-withal to be generous; generosity causes others to speak well of one, and that confers blessings, the realization of which is wealth. Honor and power are the same thing. One gains it by generosity, hence from wealth, and by meeting other obligations. Power is the result of participation in society. Generosity is an obligation and feasts are reciprocal.

This ideology has no ethical dimension, except in the most rudimentary sense in which ethics retains its meaning as what is 'customary.' Ethics, custom, religion, law are all one, *yî lî*, possibly from Chinese, or related to it. It is an ideology of power and how to acquire it. There is no ethical dimension that concerns the uses of power except that one uses it to defend oneself against other powerful beings, all of which are of the same kind whether they be visible or invisible, alive or dead.

This ideology is acted out in ritual. The ritual "communicates" nothing special, except that there are misfortune and power. There are three economic contexts for this ideology and its concomitant rituals: highland remote from markets, highland close to markets, and lowland. Where there is open access to wealth in the highlands, this ideology informs and accompanies egalitarian social forms; where there is not, it informs and accompanies hierarchic social forms.

There is no stratification, unequal access to resources (Fried 1967), in any of the hierarchic or egalitarian highland systems. This characteristic is what is at stake in the shift from Kachin to Shan, the shift from kin obligations to aristocrat-dependent or "landlord-tenant" relationships as Leach (1954: 288) styles them. Maran (1967: 139) points out that when Kachin move from lowland feudatory Kachin groups modeled themselves on Shan and return to highland groups, their highland relatives ritually purify them to remove from them the taint of Shan witchcraft and to return them to the sphere of the Kachin. To be stratified is to be non-Kachin.

Power is attributed to the source of wealth. If the source of wealth is personal productivity, there is an egalitarian system. If one inherits claims to wealth, then power is also heritable in a hierarchic system.

Power is a central axiom in both upland and lowland world views. In both systems power is crucial for defining the status of humans and other beings. Claims to power must be validated through public generosity. The use of wealth to validate claims to power through generosity returns blessings that produce more wealth. In the highlands, beings are compared with respect to power, but in the lowlands these comparisons form a universal hierarchy into which all beings fit.

In the lowlands the realities of political systems and political power are so different that there are transformations of the ideology of power. Political power rests on the control of productive resources, which rests ultimately on coercion and force (Fried 1967). One has access to productive resources by virtue of social relationships to those who have sufficient coercive power to make good claims to ownership of resources. Thus, any person's power is a consequence of social relationships with more powerful others. State systems that order social realities of stratified societies invariably develop rhetorics of justification for power relationships, often in religious terms. In lowland Southeast Asia, Buddhism has provided such a rhetoric for a variety of state systems. Thus, one can see the unity among all mainland Southeast Asian ideological systems based on concepts of personal power and its origin as they play out in different economic and political forms—highland and lowland, stratified and unstratified, hierarchic and egalitarian.

Acknowledgments

The fieldwork on which this paper is based was financed by a contract from the U. S. Army Medical Research and Development Command, Office of the Surgeon General. The fieldwork was conducted between November 1968 and September 1970.

References

Bernatzik, H. A.
1970.   *Akha and Miao*. Translated by Nagler. New Haven: Human Relations Area Files Press.

Dessaint, A. Y.
1971a.   "Lisu Annotated Bibliography." *Behavior Science Notes* 6: 71-94.

1971b.   "Lisu Migration in the Thai Highlands." *Ethnology* 10: 248-346.

Durkheim, E.
1964 (1916). *The Elementary Forms of the Religious Life*. London: Allen and Unwin.

Durrenberger, E. Paul
1974.   "The Regional Context of the Economy of a Lisu Village in Northern Thailand." *Southeast Asia* 3: 569-575.

1975a.   "Lisu Shamans and some General Questions." *Journal of the Steward Anthropological Society* 7: 1-20.

1975b.   "The Lisu Concept of the Soul." *Journal of the Siam Society* 63: 63-71.

1975c.   "A Soul's Journey." *Asian Folklore Studies* 34: 35-50.

1975d.   "Lisu Occult Roles." *Bijdragen tot de Taal-, Land-, en Volkenkunde* 131: 138-205.

1976a.   "Lisu Curing: A Case History." *Bulletin of the History of Medicine* 50: 356-371.

1976b.   "A Lisu Shamanistic Seance." *Journal of the Siam Society* 64: 151-160.

1976c.   "The Economy of a Lisu Village." *American Ethnologist* 3: 633-644.

1976d.   "A Program for Computing Sahlin's Social Profile of Domestic Production and Related Statistics." *Behavior Science Research* 11: 19-23.

1976e.   "Law and Authority in a Lisu Village: Two Cases." *Journal of Anthropological Research* 32: 301-325.

1977a.   "Of Lisu Dogs and Lisu Spirits." *Folklore* (London) 88: 61-63.

1977b.   "Lisu Etiological Categories." *Bijdragen tot de Taal-, Land-, en Volkenkunde* 133: 90-99.

1979a.   "Misfortune and Therapy among the Lisu of Northern Thailand." *Anthropological Quarterly* 52: 447-458.

1979b.   "Rice Production in a Lisu Village." *Journal of Southeast Asian Studies* 10: 139-145.

1980.   "Belief and the Logic of Lisu Spirits." *Bijdragen tot de Taal-, Land-, en Volkenkunde* 136: 21-40.

1982.   "An Analysis of Lisu Symbolism, Economics, and Cognition." *Pacific Viewpoint* 23: 127-145.

1984.   "Operationalizing Chayanov." In *Chayanov, Peasants, and Economic Anthropology,* edited by E. Paul Durrenberger, 39-50. San Francisco: Academic Press.

1986.   "Chiefly Consumption in Commonwealth Iceland." Paper presented to the 1986 meeting of the Society for Economic Anthropology, Urbana, Illinois.

Durrenberger, E. Paul and N. Tannenbaum
in press. *Analytic Perspectives on Shan Agriculture and Village Economics.* Yale University Southeast Asia Monograph Series, no. 37. New Haven: Yale University.

Forrest, G.
1908.   "Journey on Upper Salwin, October-December, 1905." *Geographical Journal* 32: 239-166.

Fried, M.
1967.   *The Evolution of Political Society.* New York: Random House.

Goullart, P.
1955.   *The Forgotten Kingdom.* London: Murray.

Hinton, P.
1969.   "Introduction." In *Tribesmen and Peasants in North Thailand*, edited by P. Hinton, 1-11. Chiang Mai: Tribal Research Centre.

Keen, F. G. B.
1970.   *Upland Tenure and Land Use in North Thailand*. Bangkok: The SEATO Cultural Programme.

Kirsch, A. T.
1973.   *Feasting and Social Oscillation: Religion and Society in Upland Southeast Asia*. Cornell University Southeast Asia Program Data Paper, no. 92. Ithaca: Southeast Asia Program, Cornell University.

Leach, E. R.
1954.   *Political Systems of Highland Burma*. Boston: Beacon.

Lehman, F. K.
1963.   *The Structure of Chin Society*. Urbana: University of Illinois Press.

1967.   "Ethnic Categories in Burma and the Theory of Social Systems." In *Southeast Asian Tribes, Minorities, and Nations*, edited by Peter Kunstadter, 93-124. Princeton: Princeton University Press.

Maran, La Raw
1967.   "Toward a Basis for Understanding the Minorities in Burma: The Kachin Example." In *Southeast Asian Tribes, Minorities, and Nations*, edited by Peter Kunstadter, 125-146.   Princeton: Princeton University Press.

McCoy, A.
1973.   *The Politics of Heroin in Southeast Asia*. New York: Harper and Row.

Rose, A. and C. Brown
1911.   "Lisu (Yawin) Tribes of the Burma-China Frontier." *Memoirs of the Royal Asiatic Society of Bengal* 3: 249-276.

Sahlins, M.
1972.   *Stone Age Economics*. Chicago: Aldine-Atherton.

Seidenfaden, E.
1967.   *The Thai Peoples*. Bangkok: The Siam Society.

Sperber, D.
1974.   *Rethinking Symbolism*. New York: Cambridge University Press.

Spiro, M.
1966.　"Religion:　Problems in Definition and Explanation." In *Anthropological Approaches to the Study of Religion*, edited by M. Banton, 85-126. London: Tavistock.

Tannenbaum, N.
1984.　"The Misuse of Chayanov: 'Chayanov's Rule' and Empiricist Bias in Anthropology." *American Anthropologist* 86: 927-942.

ECONOMY, POLITY, AND COSMOLOGY IN THE AO NAGA MITHAN FEAST

Mark R. Woodward

In 1939, on the eve of the Second World War, Edmund Leach set out for Burma intent on conducting a Malinowskian functionalist analysis of a Kachin community. He was able to spend only seven months in the village selected as the object of this study. Leach spent most of the next five years as an officer in the Burma army losing all of his field notes "as the result of enemy action" (Leach 1954: 312). This loss motivated his turn to the comparative and historical study of Kachin culture and political organization. The result was *Political Systems of Highland Burma*, which changed the direction of British social anthropology and established a research agenda that has shaped the ways in which anthropologists have viewed the tribal societies of upland Southeast Asia for more than thirty years.

Leach rejected the diffusionist orientation of previous studies of upland Southeast Asian cultures (Dalton 1872, Hutton 1921a, 1921b) as well as the equilibrium models of his teachers. As an alternative he proposed a model in which ethnic identity, social and political structure oscillate in response to shifting ecological conditions. He understands ritual as a mode of symbolic communication, the purpose of which is to make statements about the social and political status of individuals and social groups (1954: 12-16).

Most subsequent analyses of upland Southeast Asian cultures take Leach's theories as a point of departure. While Durrenberger (1979, 1980, 1982), Friedman (1979), Lehman (1963), Maran (1967), and Nugent (1982) have shown that Leach's reliance on strictly ecological variables is misplaced—and that such factors as the opium trade, proximity to lowland civilizations, and trade patterns are also critical variables—their analyses are, to a greater or lesser degree, influenced by Leach's pioneering work. Even Kirsch (1973), who emphasizes cosmological dimensions of upland religions, argues that economic and ecological variables account for the distribution of hierarchical and non-hierarchical social systems.

Leach (1954: 291-292, and again in 1964: xv) suggested that more attention should be devoted to the rich ethnographic literature on the Naga tribes of the Assam-Burma border region. Friedman (1975, 1979) is the only contemporary scholar to have made serious use of these materials. While he shows that Naga political and religious systems resemble those of the Chin and Kachin, Friedman's analysis retains Leach's materialist assumptions. He treats ideology as a constant, arguing that variant social formations are determined by a calculus of ecological variables including soil fertility, rainfall, and population density. He associates rich environments with hierarchical political systems and degraded environments with egalitarian systems. He also argues that concern with communal prosperity is among the principal components of religion in hierarchically organized tribal societies, but that it is not found among the "egalitarian" Naga (Friedman 1979: 227).

In a recent paper, Lehman (1977) questions the explanatory power of ecological models. In a discussion of the nature of "sin" he observes that among the Kachin, "the system of social categories narrowly construed is not an ultimate prime; that the social categories are deeply informed by, say, metaphysical considerations" (Lehman 1977: 230). He argues that the principal problem with Leach's analysis is that he "never goes deeply enough into the structure of Kachin ideas about crucial relationships between man and the other world" (Lehman: 231). He concludes that the analysis of native intellectual and philosophical traditions is a necessary precondition for understanding what is conventionally termed social structure. This paper explores the implications of this theory for the analysis of ritual exchange among the Ao Naga. Building on Lehman's studies of the Chin (1963) and Kachin (1977) and recent theoretical works by Bourdieu (1977) and Godelier (1986), I argue that religious beliefs concerning magical potency and the economic efficacy of ritual are not, as Leach suggests, statements about social relations. Rather they are the primary forces shaping political structure and economic behavior in the context of ecological conditions broadly conceived and culturally interpreted.

This paper examines ethnographic literature concerning cosmological, economic, and political dimensions of the Ao Naga feasts of merit.[1] It focuses on the symbolism and meanings of the mithan (*Bos frontalis*) sacrifice—the mithan being a type of horned buffalo found in Southeast Asia—that culminates in a graded series of increasingly expensive and cosmologically potent feasts. I will be particularly concerned with the manner in which the seemingly contradictory ideologies of personal status aggrandizement and collective fertility are articulated in and mitigated through ritual performance. It is shown that ceremonial exchange is predicated on a cosmological order presupposing a recursive exchange relationship between humans and ancestor worlds as the prime determinant of wealth and status, and that the relative ability of individuals to contribute to communal prosperity is central to political competition. Paradoxically, belief in the efficacy of ritual as a means of acquiring personal wealth and establishing communal prosperity is among the factors limiting the accumulation of wealth and the emergence of class stratification.

The Ao are located in the western Naga Hills, adjacent to the plains of Assam. Like those of other tribal societies of upland Southeast Asia, Ao economic and political systems include symbiotic relationships with lowland civilizations. Prior to the advent of colonial rule this relationship included both trade and raiding, both of which were dominated by a small number of large villages. The most powerful villages received land grants from the Assam *rajas* in return for which they refrained from raiding lowland market towns. Trade and warfare enabled the Ao to obtain iron, salt, shells, and firearms and provided a market for hill products including betel *(pan)*, cotton, and hemp. It also played a role in the feasting system. Ordinary cattle were obtained in the plains, while mithan were purchased from tribes located in the interior of the Naga Hills. Despite these economic relationships, Ao religion does not seem to have been influenced by Assamese Hinduism.

Mills (1926: 257) describes feasts of merit as the central components of Ao religious and political life. Here it is shown that they can be understood only in the context of an analysis of diverse fields of meaning and social relations of which agricultural production, relations of political inequality, kinship, and cosmology are the most significant.

Ecology and Agricultural Production

Friedman (1979: 216-246) speaks of ecological degradation as the primary material force shaping Naga culture. However, despite a relatively dense population, this condition does not appear to be the case in the Ao country.[2] Mills observes that

> the long and gentle slopes with their thick covering of soil give him excellent crops, and, though times of scarcity occur, real famine is rare or unknown...the Ao is careful to leave enough trees standing to regenerate the jungle, and thereby enjoys land which is no nearer worked out now than it was at the beginning. (1926: 107-108)

While most land is privately owned, there is no shortage. The average fallow period ranges from eight to fifteen years, which compares favorably with that of the Chin and Kachin (see Friedman 1979: 79-85).

Rice is the primary crop. It is also a medium of exchange, the rate for a day's labor being approximately six pounds (Mills 1926: 400).[3] Data on crop yields are not available, but it is clear that there are substantial surpluses. Mills (1926: 107) reports that a truly wealthy man is one with so much rice that it spoils in his granary. Surpluses can be depleted only through ritual redistribution, because to sell rice is a sign of poverty. In the feasting cycle large quantities of rice are eaten, and even more used to prepare beer.[4] Because feasting transforms material wealth into prestige and magical potency (both of which are sources of future wealth), it enables the elite to disperse accumulated surplus without loss of status.

Rice can be loaned at interest rates of up to one hundred percent. Since loans must be repaid in kind, large amounts of paddy accumulate in the granaries of the village elite. The poor are caught in a cycle of debt,

123

being able to grow only enough to repay loans from the previous year. Families who are unable to repay their debts are enslaved. Other slaves are purchased from neighboring tribes. Slaves are used as body guards and agricultural laborers (Mills 1926: 210), and that contributes to the further concentration of wealth to the extent that it allows for more intensive cultivation and increased military power.

Political Organization

Ao political organization can be located approximately at the midpoint of the autocratic-egalitarian continuum of Southeast Asian tribal systems. Unlike the *gumchying gumtsa* Kachin described by Maran (1967), the Ao do not have autocratic chiefs ruling fixed territories. But unlike the egalitarian Lisu mentioned by Durrenberger (1976), they recognize hereditary status positions. While there is a fixed, kinship-based system of social stratification, competition for political power is open to all except slaves.

Villages include as many as six hundred households and are governed by one or more councils *(minden)*. Council membership is determined by consensus, though certain clans, but not individuals, have hereditary rites to particular offices. Wealth, a reputation as a warrior, and participation in the feasting system are the principal criteria for selection. Councilors "eat" fines they assess and receive portions of all animals sacrificed at feasts of merit and other communal ceremonies.[5]

These shares of meat are important status markers. Mills (1926: 182-184) mentions that a man's status may be accurately assessed by the size of his share, and that this action is a frequent cause of disputes. There is also a complex system of ornaments and ceremonial cloths, some of which are the prerogative of specific clans and others of which may be earned either by performance of feasts of merit or taking of heads. Of these the most valuable is a cloth that may only be worn by those who have offered the mithan sacrifice and whose fathers and grandfathers were also feast-givers (Mills 1926: 36). The value of this cloth indicates that the status and magical potency accruing to a local lineage segment for the performance of the feast last for a minimum of three generations.

Serious disputes are settled by the most important councilors of powerful villages who back their decisions with armed force. Mills (1926: 191-193) refers to these men as "judges" and observes that those who are overly rapacious or heavy-handed may be killed or banished. Ao judges, unlike the chiefs of the Kachin or the neighboring Konyak Naga, do not enjoy special religious prerogatives and do not claim to monopolize access to the supernatural realms. As Friedman (1975) observes, putative control of supernatural power is the prime ideological component of chieftainship. It is then logical to conclude that Ao judges cannot establish themselves as chiefs, because the notion that any single individual or lineage can monopolize the available sources of supernatural power is absent from Ao cosmological thought.

While the Ao do not have chiefs, they recognize the principle of aristocracy. The Ao maintain that the *pongen* phratry corresponds with, and is the "brother" of, the Konyak *ang* or aristocratic clan.[6] As such, the phratry members are entitled to a disproportionate share of council seats and special ornaments. Members of other phratries must perform feasts of merit to wear ornaments to which the *pongen* have an inherent right. Despite their aristocratic status and the economic advantage it entails, the *pongen* are unable to monopolize either the material or cosmological resources required for the establishment of an autocratic political system. Supra-local political systems are also based on the council system. Mills reports that the entire Ao country is dominated by a small number of large villages that extract tribute from their smaller neighbors. In such cases the village council "eats" and redistributes the tribute. Thus, we have the formation of "realms" similar to those of Kachin *gumchying gumtsa* chiefs, but without the institution of territorially-based chieftainship.

Kinship and Marriage Alliance

Levi-Strauss (1969: 292-311) and Friedman (1979: 241) observe that agnatic descent rather than the wife-giver/wife-taker distinction predominates in the specification of Ao kin terms and in social relations. Calculations based on descent, for example, are employed to determine terms of address even for immediate affines (Mills 1926: 175). While the ethnography is not sufficiently clear to allow for a completely unproblematical analysis of Ao kinship, Mills' descriptions of marriage, and of the roles of affines, agnates, and "formal friends" in the feasts of merit indicate that the system is based on two basic concepts: the maximal extension of agnatic relationships and asymmetric alliance.

Ao kinship differs from that of the Kachin and Chin primarily in that clans are important social groups.[7] Each clan has a distinct origin myth, specific political rights, food, and other taboos. There are three named sets of "brother" clans that are referred to in the literature as phratries. Phratries, like clans, are ranked with respect to all of the principle status gradients of Ao culture.[8] Rank does not, however, offer advantage or rights in the feasting system, which is open to married men of every clan.

Clans are strictly exogamous, but are not units of marriage alliance. Marriage alliances are contracted by minimal lineage segments. The fact that Ao bride prices are extremely low indicates that marriage does not play a major role in establishing rank or political power. Wife-givers and wife-takers do, however, have clearly distinct roles in feasts of merit. The feast-giver's wife's father receives a large share of meat, including one of the haunches of the principal sacrificial animal. Wife-takers are required to do much of the manual labor, dance, and sing the praises of the feast-giver. In return they receive minor shares of meat.

The institution of "formal friendship" is the clearest example of the extension of agnatic relationships. The most important formal friends are the *atombu* and *ashibu*. The *atombu* is a man of a different phratry and a different village, that is, one who is both a potential affine and a potential enemy. The relationship is established through the exchange of pork and cattle. Payments must also be made to clan members and to wife-takers, seemingly to compensate them for acquiring an important "agnate." These relationships are renewed in each generation, permanently linking two local lineage segments. The children of *atombu* treat each other as agnates and are forbidden to marry. It is also forbidden to take the head of one's *atombu* in time of war. This institution may, therefore, be interpreted as an attempt to extend effective agnatic ties to members of a totally unrelated clan. Relationships with the *ashibu* are similar, though this individual is a man of a different phratry, but not a different village. While in one sense he is "closer," the *ashibu* is not considered to be as important as the *atombu*.

The significance of formal friendship is revealed most fully in the feast of merit. The *atombu* and *ashibu* are the ones who render the greatest aid to the feast-giver and in return receive large shares of the meat. They, rather than "genuine" agnates, stand by his side as the sacrificial victims are led to slaughter and help to recite prayers to the feast-giver's ancestors (Mills 1926: 257-261). "Genuine" agnates receive shares of meat and are among the guests at feasts of merit, but do little, if anything, to aid in its performance. These data strongly suggests that there is intense political competition within the clan and that feasts of merit are intended to establish agnatic, rather than affinal ranking. In other words, the position of a lineage segment within the clan is determined by feasting rather than genealogical position. This view is supported by the fact that the Ao do not pay high bride prices and that it is, therefore, impossible to receive a return on one's investment through the alliance system. The financial "pay off" from feasts of merit comes rather from the ability to secure a seat on the village council. This situation can be obtained only by establishing one's position within the clan, at the direct expense of one's "real" agnates. Because wife-givers and wife-takers have distinct roles to play in the feast (as recipients of the haunches of mithan and dancers respectively) they cannot assist the feast-giver with his role. Agnates other than members of his minimal lineage segment have nothing to gain, and potentially much to lose, from the feast-giver's enhanced status. Formal friends are brought in as outsiders, such as men who are not in any sense in competition with the feast-giver, to help with ceremonial duties.

The Cosmological Foundations of Ao Feasting

The preceding discussion indicates that feasts of merit are among the means through which status and political office are achieved and that it is only through feasting that accumulated surplus can be redistributed and dissipated. The economic and political analysis of ritual does not, however, reveal much concerning the cultural and intellectual concepts motivating its performance. The meaning of the feasts of merit, as opposed to their political and economic functions, can be understood only in the context of an analysis of the cosmological order it presupposes.

The Ao cosmos includes the earth, which is inhabited by humans and spirits and a series of skies and underworlds. Sacrifices, including feasts of merit, are offered to the spirits and ancestors of the sky. The prosperity that is the result of these sacrifices rises through the underworld in the form of agricultural fertility. Paradoxically, the underworld is also understood as the abode of the ancestors (Mills 1926: 226-228). Recent studies of Naga (and other tribal Southeast Asian) cosmologies have shown that this seeming paradox derives from the fact that relationships between the earth, sky, and underworld are structured by the principle of asymmetric alliance and the belief that nonhuman realms are populated by the spirits of the dead (Loeffler 1968, Friedman 1975). The ancestors of the sky-world occupy a position structurally analogous to that of wife-givers, while those of the underworld are analogous to wife-takers.[9] There must be two lands of the dead because the living must have both superior and inferior extrahuman relationships. As Lehman (1977: 237) observes, this is a paradox of "cosmic proportions." It lies at the heart of cosmo-logical speculation throughout upper Burma and Assam, motivating both seemingly contradictory beliefs concerning the location of the ancestors and a great variety of surface cosmological forms. This complex of belief is also illustrative of the interdependence of inferior and superior allies, that is, to receive material goods one must have first received symbolic or magical qualities, which may be obtained only by giving material goods.

In general, life in the land of the dead is said to be similar to that on earth, except that there is no sexual intercourse and no birth. People arrive in the village of the dead by following the path of their agnatic ancestors. The rich are rich in the land of the dead and the poor remain so. Wealth and status are functions of the number of feasts of merit one has performed as the sacrificial animals join the feast-giver on the road. Similarly, victims of headhunting become slaves in the afterlife. Death in the land of the dead results in movement to yet another sky or underworld, or simply to the termination of existence.

One major difference between this world and the next is that there are chiefs in the ancestral realm. The "king" of the underworld acts as a judge, punishing thieves and other wrongdoers. Anungtsungba (Lord of the Heavens) is a chief in every sense of the word. The dead are required to build his house and dance at his feasts. He is held to be responsible for the prosperity of the living, and, according to Clark (1911), assigns each person a "fate" *(tiya)* at birth. The *tiya* is one of the sky-people and may cause illness and misfortune as well as prosperity. In the case of childlessness or serious illness, offerings are made to both the chief of the dead and to the *tiya* (Mills 1926: 236).

The sky-world is also the source of magical fertility *(aren)*. The term is derived from the root *ren*, "to increase" (Clark 1911: 113), and is perhaps the most important concept in Ao religion.[10] It is a spiritual substance or quality that is held to be inherent in ancestors, rich men, and other superiors. Mills (1926: 380-381) reports that feasts of merit, ancestral offerings, and most of the agricultural ceremonies are in some way intended to acquire or mobilize *aren*. It is believed to be the single most important determinant of crop yields, human and animal fertility.

The Ao concept of *aren* resembles what Bourdieu (1977: 171-182) terms "symbolic capital." He observes that prestige, magical power, and other things acquired through ritual, magic, and other religious means may be converted into economic resources and that symbolic capital is among the most important resources in premodern economies. He argues that a spiritual element is introduced into exchange relationships to veil the calculation of economic advantage on which they are based and to present exchange objects as "pure gifts" in the Maussian sense. In general, his analysis captures much of the ideological foundation and practical logic of Ao ritual. There are, however, two crucial differences. The first is that the Ao do not make any attempt to veil the economic dimension of ritual performance. The second is that Bourdieu pays insufficient attention to the cosmological foundations of symbolic capital. *Aren*, for example, is not understood simply as a means of mobilizing human labor and material resources. Rather, it is a supernatural substance that is thought to directly and causally influence crop yields and the prosperity of the individual or social group that controls it. The salient theoretical point here is that from the perspective of Ao culture there is nothing symbolic about supernatural beings and powers. They are known to exist and to play major roles in human affairs. Consequently, rituals that are intended to produce *aren* cannot be understood as symbolic statements about social relations. They are, again from an Ao perspective, totally pragmatic attempts to establish agricultural fertility and other forms of prosperity.

While the sky is the source of *aren*, the prosperity it produces rises upward through the earth. Mithan skulls and human heads (both sent to the sky) are the sources of *aren*, while cane shoots and sword beans (both associated with the earth) are the symbols of material prosperity.[11] These earth symbols are tied to sacrificial mithan and prayers are offered so that the feast-giver and his children will "grow and flourish like a cane shoot which can push its way up past sticks and stones" (Mills 1926: 372). More than anything else, this religious complex reveals the nature of relationships between underworld, earth, and sky. The sky is the source of magical fertility *(aren)*, but this potency is converted into material wealth only by way of the underworld. All of the major sacrifices are sent to the sky with the hope that prosperity will rise through the earth. Agricultural rites transfer *aren* from the dwelling house to the temporary field house and from there to the growing crops (see Mills 1926: 107-123).[12]

The Ao view of the relationship between earth, sky, and underworld is, then, precisely the same as that described by Maran (personal communication) for a Kachin lineage and its wife-givers and wife-takers:[13]

> The *mayu* (wife-givers) are the breath of life;
> the *mayu* are the main source of our children;
> the *mayu* are the source of refreshment,
> and by making marriage we are refreshed.
> The *dama* (wife-takers) are those who put wealth in the hand.

The sky is, with respect to the earth, a superior and the "source of refreshment"—in this case *aren*. As such, payments in the form of feasts of merit must be made to the inhabitants of the sky-world. The underworld is inferior and the direct source of material goods—in this case crops.

The religious significance of the mithan is closely tied to the concept of *aren*. Loeffler (1968) has argued that the mithan, together with fish and the Great Indian Hornbill, are the master symbols of Naga cultures. The fish represents the underworld, the hornbill, the sky. Loeffler sees the mithan as the primary earth symbol. Among the Ao, however, the "earth" is further subdivided into a number of "subcosmic" domains each with its own animal symbol. Villages (culture) are opposed to jungle (nature). Fields are a liminal category in that they are ritually incorporated into the human realm in planting rituals (Mills 1926: 112), but are allowed to return to jungle.

Mithan represent a second, permanently liminal category. They are only semi-domesticated and live in light forests at high elevations. They are located between earth and sky, and between culture and nature. They return to villages periodically, usually to find salt, for which they have unusual cravings. They are sacrificed, but never slaughtered simply for food. In feasts of merit they move between earth and sky and, owing to the interdependent nature of alliance, are the prime source of wealth and status in both realms.

The dominant creature in each of these three permanent domains (jungle, village, and highlands)—tigers, humans, and mithan—are thought to have souls and to be sources of *aren*. The tiger is dangerous and is closely associated with sorcery (Mills 1926: 247). As such it is not included in the feasts of merit. The mithan, on the other hand, carries strong

129

associations with agriculture and fertility. Ao mythology states that rice was originally discovered in the stomach of a sacrificed mithan and that magically potent stones may be found in their bodies (Mills 1926: 290, 313). Because they have souls, headhunting rites can be performed for any of these creatures. In this way their *aren* is captured and made available to the lineage and village of the hunter.[14]

This basic complex of religious belief is shared by all of the Naga. The Ao have a more elaborate cosmological view of the mithan according to which those of the sky are the souls of humans, while those of the earth are the souls of the sky-people (ancestors). The sacrifice of a mithan in either domain causes the death of the human whose soul it is. The owner of one's mithan soul is the *tiya* (birth-fate) and is among the most important sources of *aren*. A person with a rich *tiya* becomes wealthy and gives many feasts. Similarly, one's poverty may be attributed to that of the *tiya*. The relationship between earth, sky, and underworld is systemic because the wealth of the *tiya* depends on the number of sacrifices it offered as a human (Mills 1926: 223-226), which in turn is a function of the amount of material prosperity rising through the underworld. The mithan is, therefore, both a form of wealth and the means through which wealth is transferred to the sky-world and transformed into *aren*. The fact that the sacrifice of a mithan necessarily entails the death of a human in the other world is expressive of the tension inherent between superior and inferior in systems of asymmetric alliance—if there is no status difference, there can be no exchange, but if the status difference becomes too great (in this case through feasting) the relationship cannot be maintained. The death of a mithan, then, entails the establishment of one relationship at the cost of the cancellation of another. Mithans must die to enhance the status of the feast-giver. But this results in the death of a sky person who is a source of *aren* for some other human. Similarly, sky-people obtain *aren* by sacrificing mithan that are the souls of the living. Consequently, any increase of status in either domain, and with it the acquisition of *aren*, results in death in the other domain and a decline in the amount of *aren* available to those with whom the feast-giver is in competition. As Lehman (personal communication) puts it, "one up implies one down."

The systemic nature of the earth/sky/underworld relationship also allows us to explain the economic logic of Ao sacrifices. Mills (1926: 260) and Majumder (n.d.: 27) observe that while there is a minimum number of animals required for each feast of merit, there is no maximum. Majumder (n.d.: 27) states that although only one mithan is required, many feast-givers sacrifice as many as twelve. Mills (1926: 260) describes one feast in which forty mithan were slaughtered. Mithan weigh up to a thousand pounds. Given the fact that Nagas eat almost everything except the bones, it is reasonable to suggest that one mithan would yield six to seven hundred pounds of meat. In addition to the mithan, numerous pigs, fowl, and as much as twenty-five tons of rice are required for a large feast

(Majumder n.d.: 27). Given the fact that six pounds of rice or two pounds of meat is the standard wage for a day's work (Mills 1926: 398-400), the value of a large feast of merit is enormous. Moreover, it is unlikely that the feast-giver would ever recover his expenses from bride prices or other payments. The vast sums expended in feasts of merit probably also account for Mills' (1926: 35) observation that it is rare for wealth to be preserved for more than two generations. Feasts of merit make economic "sense" only when the concept of *aren* is included in the equation. By making large sacrifices to the sky, it is hoped that a corresponding amount of prosperity will rise through the earth. This expectation is based on religious assumptions concerning the sources of prosperity and is a clear illustration of the manner in which economic behavior is influenced by cosmological thought. At the same time, it motivates the distribution of accumulated surplus and partly precludes the development of class stratification.

The Performative Structure of the Ao Mithan Feast

The mithan sacrifice may be offered only by individuals who have completed an extensive and costly series of preliminary rites. These include a series of feasts in which cattle and hogs are killed and presents of meat given to affines, agnates, and formal friends (Mills 1926: 384-88). The mithan feast itself requires at least eighteen months to prepare.

None of these preliminary rites is a sacrifice in the true sense of the word, because animals are not sent to the land of the dead. Some are economic transactions that compensate others for the fact that the feast-giver's status will soon be dramatically increased. The feast-giver virtually purchases permission to perform the mithan sacrifice from the council and from the village as a whole. By doing so, he demonstrates that he is a wealthy man and, at least potentially, a source of *aren*. Others welcome the mithan to the village and establish a social/religious bond between the animal and the feast-giver.

On the first day of the feast, a man of the feast-giver's clan who has also offered the sacrifice announces that a mithan will be tied up the following day. This is a lie intended to fool the sky-people because the animal will not actually be killed until the third day. The purpose of this lie is to prevent the sky-people from attempting to stop a sacrifice that results in the death of a mithan soul. In a more general sense, it is expressive of tension between earth and sky. While the sky is the source of *aren*, the sky-people appear to be reluctant to bestow it, or to grant the living the status resulting from the mithan sacrifice.

On the second day, the mithan is adorned with hornbill feathers, which symbolize the sky, and with cane and sword beans, which represent the fertility that rises through the earth. It is then tied to a post in the center of the village. The wife-takers of the feast-giver throw the animal to the ground, torture it, and dance on it. Agnatic kinsmen prevent them from killing it because the mithan would be angry in the next world if it died in this way (Mills 1926: 379). It is significant that wife-takers, like the sky-people, ritually attempt to stop the sacrifice. Wife-takers must supply most of the labor for the feast, only to see the status of their superiors increased. But while superior sky-people are tricked into ignoring the sacrifice, inferior wife-takers are physically prevented from harming the mithan. The result is often a general brawl. Next the animal is led to the feast-giver's house where the feast-giver apologizes to it by stating that he did not order the torture. In this and in other instances, he presents himself as the friend and protector of the sacrificial animal, feeding it and giving it salt and water.

On the third day, formal friends erect a forked post in front of the feast-giver's house. The post is a "cosmic axis" linking earth and sky and is decorated with carvings of hornbills. It is through the post that the mithan will be sent to the village of the ancestors. Prayers are offered for the prosperity of the village and the wish expressed that the sacrificer will offer so many feasts that nothing will be left of the jungle but stumps.

Next, the mithan is tied to the post and prepared for sacrifice. During the afternoon, men and women of all clans dance around it. In the early evening the feast-giver and his wife, accompanied by two formal friends, present offerings representing all of the cosmic domains capable of producing wealth to the mithan. These include rice, flour, salt, water, fish, and beer. Prayers are recited in which the feast-giver "calls" the aren of his ancestors and that of the entire Ao country to his village and house. The beast is told to go and find the feast-giver's father, which indicates that agnates in the sky-world are the principal source of aren. These prayers are also illustrative of the manner in which the feast establishes rank within clans in both realms. Feasting enhances the position of the feast-giver's local lineage segment. By sending a mithan to the sky, feasts also enhance the status of his deceased agnates. Throughout this ceremony, the feast-giver's father's sister's daughters (women of wife-taking lineages) pound fermented rice to prevent evil spirits from spoiling the sacrifice.

The mithan is killed by an old man of the feast-giver's clan who has not offered the sacrifice himself and is, therefore, of low status. The feast-giver and his wife may not see the animal killed or eat any of the meat. It is possible to suggest that the feast-giver must disassociate himself from the death of the mithan because it has been ritually incorporated into his village, clan, and household. Killing the animal is both dangerous and taboo, in the same sense that killing, or taking the head of a close agnate is. Because the clan is the primary focus of the ritual, the mithan must be killed by an agnate. A poor old man has, at least as far as status is concerned, nothing to lose and is paid for his services.

After the sacrifice, men of the feast-giver's clan dance with women of their wife-giving clans until dawn. The next morning, two of the clan priests climb onto the roof of the feast-giver's house and call like hornbills to announce the sacrifice to the sky-people. Then the meat is divided. One of the front quarters is given to wife-takers and both hind legs to the feast-giver's immediate wife-givers. The remainder and other presents of meat are given to agnates and to representatives of every clan in the village. The skull of the mithan is then cleaned and hung in the men's house where it remains until the next harvest. On the final day the feast-giver and his wife perform purification rites. A large pig is then killed in front of the granary and prayers are recited for *aren* to replenish the feast-giver's supply of surplus rice.

This concludes the mithan sacrifice. It does not, however, terminate the feast-giver's relationship with the mithan. During the harvest ritual he repeats the prayers and offerings made to the beast and moves its skull to his own house. These rites are repeated every year and constitute a continuous source of *aren*. Skulls are passed from one generation to the next, leading to the accumulation of magical potency in localized lineage segments.

Feasts of Merit as Communal Fertility Rites

The primary purpose of the feast of merit is to enhance the prosperity and status of the feast-giver and his immediate agnates. Feasting rather than genealogical position establishes rank within clans. The feast also enhances the position of a corresponding group in the sky-world as material wealth rises from the earth to the sky. However, prayers recited at the feast indicate that communal fertility is also an important concern and that the status of the feast-giver derives in part from his ability to serve as a source of *aren* for the clan and the village. The fact that the mithan skull hangs in the men's house for a year indicates that the feast-giver must be as generous with the newly acquired *aren* as he was with the meat and beer through which it was acquired.

The communal dimension of feasting is clearly articulated in village agricultural rites that call the *aren* of the rich and of other villages. Mills (1926: 112, 257) observes that superiors in general and rich men in particular are obligated to serve as sources of *aren* for the community. Normally an entire village cultivates a single block of land. After it has been cleared and ceremonies conducted to drive off any wild jungle spirits, each man constructs a field house. The field house serves as a ceremonial center, resting place, and threshing floor. Here Mills emphasizes the contribution of wealthy men to communal fertility:

> It is also important that the rich men of the village should build their field houses first, and the poor men later. This is because rich men are naturally endowed with *aren*—the curious quality of innate prosperity in

which the Ao believes so strongly. This virtue, by building their field houses first, they will impart to the whole block of cultivation. (1926: 112)

Before the fields can be planted, the village priests collect seeds from rich men, which are thought to contain great quantities of *aren*. These are carefully planted in an enclosed area just outside of the village. Pigs are sacrificed, and the meat is shared by members of the village council (Mills 1926: 113). The purpose of this rite is to imbue the entire block of cultivation with *aren* and to enhance the fertility of the village as a whole.

There is a clear connection between the performance of the mithan sacrifice and communal prosperity. If it is not offered in a given year, the village as a collectivity sacrifices a bull to acquire *aren* and enhance fertility (Mills 1926: 254). Ceremonies performed in times of scarcity or when crops are poor provide an even clearer example. At such times a bamboo framework is built outside of the village and covered with the skulls of sacrificed mithan and captured human heads. Prayers are then recited and the *aren* of particularly wealthy men called to the village (Mills 1926: 288).

Given the Ao belief that feasts of merit are among the prime sources of *aren* and wealth, it is reasonable to suggest that these collective rites are attempts to obtain the *aren* produced by previous feasts. Thus, while the primary purposes of feasting are individual status aggrandizement and the acquisition of *aren*, it also enhances the fertility of every social group involved in the rite. It transforms material wealth (which is private) into a store of magical potency upon which all participants may draw. It transfers *aren* from the sky to the earth and fixes it in all of the social groups participating in the feast. Given the nature of Ao cosmology, this is the only way in which future prosperity can be guaranteed. Feasting also enhances the feast-giver's position in the after-life and establishes him as a potentially potent source of *aren* for future generations. Viewed from the perspective of Ao cosmology, the system "works" to counterbalance individual concern with status with the common good. Status can be enhanced only in the context of rites that establish communal prosperity, which balance status and *aren* losses suffered by others. On the other hand, communal prosperity can be maintained only through the establishment of a status/*aren* hierarchy.

Conclusions: Feasting, Ideology, and Economic Behavior

The feasting system is the primary arena for status competition in Ao culture. Its principle political goal is to establish the position of a lineage segment within the larger clan. The exploitation of relationships with wife-givers and wife-takers is not an end unto itself, but rather a way to raise one's status within the agnatic clan. Yet, the basis of status is cosmological and religious. It is only through the mithan sacrifice and the acquisition of magical potency *(aren)* that surplus production may be transformed into social position. This magical potency is, in turn, understood as the basis of communal as well as individual prosperity. The cost of feasts of merit and their seemingly limited economic returns speak for the strength of Ao belief in *aren* and in the power of ideology as a determinant of both social organization and economic behavior.

The most important conclusion to be drawn from this analysis is that upland Southeast Asian cosmologies, rituals, and social systems cannot be understood simply as the output of a calculus of crop yields, ecological conditions, population density, and other material variables as Leach (1954) and Friedman (1979) maintain.

Friedman's (1979) structural Marxist study of political and religious variation is perhaps the most ambitious and certainly the most complex comparative work on upland Southeast Asia. Yet, the analysis of Ao religion and social organization presented here raises serious questions about Friedman's conclusions and the theoretical assumptions on which they are based. Friedman argues that ethnographic variation in the Assam-Burma border area is the output of a complex calculus of soil fertility, population density, rainfall, and other ecological variables. He presents a detailed model of the structural transformations linking Kachin, Chin, Naga, and Wa social systems and religions. In this model a concern with communal prosperity is associated with low population density and highly stratified political systems. "Egalitarian" polities, including those of the Naga, are explained as the consequence of an ecologically driven structural devolution in which the political and religious dimensions of chiefly authority give way to a social order characterized by egalitarian clans and feasting as a "competitive affinal potlatch" that does not "represent the larger community before the spirit world in an attempt to bring on increased prosperity" (Friedman 1979: 227).

Examination of cosmological and economic foundations of ceremonial exchange and the religious significance of the mithan has shown that, at least with respect to the Ao, Friedman's contention that Naga political systems are "egalitarian" because of ecological degradation and over population is both factually incorrect and analytically simplistic. The Ao are "egalitarian" not because they cannot afford to have chiefs, but because their cosmological system does not allow any individual or social group to monopolize the available sources of magical potency. The system is "democratic" only to the extent that status and village political offices are granted to those individuals who have proven themselves to be sources of communal fertility.

Friedman makes three specific errors:

1. The Ao environment (as of 1920) is not seriously degraded and in fact produces a substantial surplus.
2. While there are no chiefs, Ao society is highly stratified, and the principle of inherited status is recognized. Moreover, the absence of genealogical ranking does not imply that the internal structure of clans is egalitarian. Ranking exists, but is based on participation in the feasting system rather than genealogical position.
3. While feasting is inherently competitive, the essence of political/ritual competition is the relative ability of individuals and local lineage segments to control and redistribute the types of magical power *(aren)* that are the basis for both individual and collective prosperity.

In a more general sense, the analysis of Ao feasting presented here indicates that the study of political and religious variation in upland Southeast Asia must balance the study of material "facts" with the investigation of ideology and meaning—and that cosmologies, rituals, and social systems cannot be reduced to, or explained solely in terms of, a calculus of crop yields and population density—even if that calculus is correct. Moreover, the economic analysis of ritual must consider not only material components of exchange relationships, but also cultural and cosmological presuppositions about the nature of economic processes and the ways in which these systems of ideas govern the use, distribution, and accumulation of material resources and labor.

Godelier (1986) has come to similar conclusions in his analysis of gender roles and male domination among the Baruya of New Guinea. He argues that in the absence of class stratification, relations of inequality are determined more by systems of ideas than by material forces. In an elegant theoretical passage he writes:

> Consequently the relation between the conceptual and the nonconceptual in the real world cannot be construed as the relation between a reflection and the reality reflected. Thought does not reflect; it gives meaning to situations born of causes and forces whose origins do not lie solely in the conscious or the unconscious. Thought invents and produces this meaning by constructing systems of interpretation which engender symbolic practices, which are themselves so many manners of organizing and legitimizing, which also produce male domination over women and thereby become social relations. It would be simple if thought could confine itself merely to reflecting or representing society, but the whole difficulty of scientifically analyzing the conceptual factor in the real world stems from the fact that thought

not only represents society but itself contributes to the
production of society. (1986: 232)

I have quoted Godelier at length because his insights are as
applicable to the study of upland Southeast Asia as they are to that of
highland New Guinea. The fact that upland Southeast Asian societies
exhibit varying degrees of social stratification does not diminish the power
of his argument. Nor do varying ecological conditions in the region.
Indeed, the analysis of Ao materials indicates that the influence of
material and ecological forces is primarily negative. Material conditions
of existence—such as rainfall, soil fertility, technology, population density,
etc.—constrain, but do not determine the social articulation of systems of
ideas. Again the comparison of the "egalitarian" Ao Naga and the
"autocratic" *gumtsa* Kachin provides a cogent example. Friedman (1979:
150-152) shows that in areas of low population density Kachin autocratic
polities are fundamentally expansionist, that is, they constantly "throw off"
new settlements into previously unsettled territory. Such a system is not
possible in the Naga hills where there is little, if any, vacant land. But this
does not mean that either system is determined by the environment or
that one can be understood as a "devolution" of the other. Indeed, the
very complexity of ethnographic and religious variation in upland
Southeast Asia seems to defy explanation in ecological terms. As Leach
(1954: 291-292) observes, the range of cultural diversity, even within a
relatively small geographic area, is enormous. What I have tried to show
in this paper is that this variation is not the product of ecological variation,
but rather of different, though closely related, ideas about the nature of
the super-natural, social life, and relations between the two. To
paraphrase Leach (1964: xv), I would suggest "that this unconventional
style of analysis" might be applied more generally in the study of the
societies, cultures, and intellectual traditions of upland Southeast Asia.

Acknowledgments

I would like to thank Cornelia Kammerer, F. K. Lehman, Juliane Schober,
and Stanley Tambiah for comments on early drafts of this paper. I would
also like to thank Sheila Lehman for invaluable data on household
consumption patterns.

Notes

1. Field work in the Naga hills has been impossible since the beginning
   of the Second World War owing to unstable political conditions.
   While I am in general agreement with Friedman's (1975) claim that it
   is not possible to differentiate sharply between economy and religion
   in these societies, his interpretation of Naga religion is simplistic at

best. The analysis presented here is based primarily on Mills' (1926) account of Ao culture and religion and assumes an "ethnographic present" of the mid-1920s. Such an interpretive enterprise is justified by the richness of the ethnography and because it has served as a source for a substantial body of comparative and theoretical work (Friedman 1975, 1979; Leach 1954; Levi-Strauss 1969; Loeffler 1968). Mills' *Ao Nagas* is the most detailed and insightful of the tribal ethnographies produced during the colonial era. In part because he did not consider himself to be a professional anthropologist and was not overly concerned with the diffussionist theories of the day, Mills presents a clear, detailed description of social life, culture, and ritual. While he does not explicitly discuss relationships between cosmology, ritual, and political organization, his ethnography provides most of the data required for a modern theoretical analysis. Moreover, the fact that most of the Ao were converted to Christianity in the 1920s and 1930s leaves his account as the only possible source of information on the traditional economic and ritual system.

2. It is extremely difficult to arrive at meaningful figures for population density in upland Southeast Asia. Computations must be based not on the total land area, which includes large amounts of uncultivated valley and steep slopes, but on land that can actually be brought into production. In 1921, approximately 30,000 Ao occupied a total area of approximately 600 square miles yielding a figure of 50 persons/square mile. The effective population density must have been considerably higher.

3. Stevenson (1943) reports that approximately five pounds of rice per day is sufficient to support a family of five. Sheila Lehman (personal communication) provides more detailed figures: two pounds/day for working adults and one for the elderly and children.

4. Fermented rice left over from beer production is used as animal feed. The animals (hogs and cattle) provide the basis for subsequent feasts.

5. In this respect councilors enjoy much the same prerogative as Kachin and other aristocratic chiefs.

6. The Konyak are among the most aristocratic of all of the hill tribes of mainland Southeast Asia. Significantly, in Konyak religion feasts of merit are replaced by calendrical fertility rites that are the exclusive prerogative of the *ang* (Fürer-Haimendorf 1969: 52-64).

7. See Lehman (1970) for an account of Chin and Kachin marriage rules.

8. Rights to council positions, cloths, and ornaments are typical status markers. Mills (1926: 164) reports that in some instances members of low-ranking phratries must perform feasts of merit to acquire ornaments that others may wear because of rank.

9. This does not imply, as Leach (1970) seems to suggest, that the sky-people are in any literal sense the wife-givers of living humans, or that cosmology is a symbolic representation of social order (see Lehman 1977). Indeed, in the case of the Ao the ideology of asymmetric alliance finds clearer expression in cosmology than it does in social relations. Nor is there anything resembling a marriage cycle in Naga cosmology. The structural parallels of the two domains are, rather, the result of the use of a common ideological principle to structure two quite different phenomena. Moreover, as Schulte Nordholt (1971) has pointed out, the existence of structural analogies does not justify the assumption of unidirectional causal relations.

10. Mills (1926: 111) was aware of the importance of *aren* in Ao culture, but not of the relationship between cosmology and marriage alliance. Hutton, in a footnote to Mill's text (1926: 257 fn. 1) compares *aren* with the polynesian concept of *mana* and with Native American religious concepts. This example is typical of his diffusionist orientation.

11. Sword beans *(Entada scandens)* are associated with fertility and used in a wide variety of rituals (see Mills 1926: 116). Mills states that the reason for their use is the extraordinary size of its seed pods.

12. The relationship between *aren* and the rice crop is very clearly articulated in Ao customs concerning the division of property in cases of divorce. The skulls of sacrificed animals and all animals that can be sacrificed remain with the husband. Rules for the division of standing crops are complex, but in all cases the husband must be allowed to reap at least one basket of rice from the vicinity of the field house "for that portion of the crop contains his *aren*" (Mills 1926: 277).

13. See Lehman (1977) for a more detailed discussion of these materials. The important point here is that the ideology (as opposed to the social forms) of Kachin marriage seem to be virtually identical with that of the Ao feasting system.

14. Head-taking ceremonies may be performed with the tail of a mithan. It is, of course, not possible to sacrifice such an animal because it has already been sent to the land of the dead by someone else. Mills reports that since the abolition of headhunting, capturing a mithan's tail entitles a young man to wear the regalia of a warrior.

References

Bourdieu, P.
1977.   *Outline of a Theory of Practice.* London: Cambridge University Press.

Clark, E.
1911.   *Ao-Naga Dictionary.* Calcutta: Baptist Mission Press.

Dalton, E.
1872.   *Descriptive Ethnography of Bengal.* Calcutta: Government of Bengal.

Durrenberger, E. Paul
1976.   "The Economy of a Lisu Village." *American Ethnologist* 3: 633-644.

1979.   "Rice Production in a Lisu Village." *Journal of Southeast Asian Studies* 10: 127-145.

1980.   "Belief and Logic of Lisu Spirits." *Bijdragen tot de Taal-, Land-, en Volkenkunde* 136: 21-40.

1982.   "An Analysis of Lisu Symbolism, Economics, and Cognition." *Pacific Viewpoint* 23: 127-145.

Friedman, J.
1975.   "Religion as Economy and Economy as Religion." *Ethnos* 40(1-4): 46-63.

1979.   *System Structure and Contradiction. The Evolution of 'Asiatic' Social Formations.* Copenhagen: The National Museum of Denmark.

Fürer-Haimendorf, C. von
1969.   *The Konyak Naga.* New York: Holt, Rinehart and Winston.

Godelier, M.
1986.   *The Making of Great Men.* London: Cambridge University Press.

Hutton, J.
1921a.   *The Angami Nagas.* London: Macmillan and Co.

1921b.   *The Sema Nagas.* London: Macmillan and Co.

Kirsch, A. T.
1973.   *Feasting and Social Oscillation: Religion and Society in Upland Southeast Asia.* Cornell University Southeast Asia Program Data

Paper, no. 92. Ithaca: Southeast Asia Program, Cornell University.

Leach, E.
1954.   *Political Systems of Highland Burma.* London: Bell.

1964.   *Political Systems of Highland Burma.* Second edition. Boston: Beacon Press.

1970.   "The Concept of Sin among the Kachin of North Burma." *Proceedings of the Eighth International Congress of Anthropological and Ethnological Sciences,* Tokyo, section S-9: 307-309.

Lehman, F. K.
1963.   *The Structure of Chin Society.* Urbana: University of Illinois Press.

1970.   "On Chin and Kachin Marriage Regulations." *Man* (N.S.) 5(1): 118-125.

1977.   "Kachin Social Categories and Methodological Sins." In *Language and Thought: Anthropological Issues,* edited by William C. McCormack and Stephen A. Wurm, 229-249. The Hague: Mouton.

Levi-Strauss, C.
1969.   *The Elementary Structures of Kinship.* Translated by Rodney Needham. Boston: Beacon Press.

Loeffler, L.
1968.   "Beast, Bird and Fish: An Essay in Southeast Asian Symbolism." In *Folk Religion and the World View in the Southwestern Pacific,* 21-33. Tokyo: Keio Institute of Cultural and Linguistic Studies, Keio University.

Majumder, S.
n.d.   *The Ao Naga.* Calcutta: By the Author.

Maran, LaRaw
1967.   "Towards a Basis for Understanding the Minorities of Burma." In *Southeast Asian Tribes, Minorities and Nations,* vol. 1, edited by P. Kunstadter, 125-146. Princeton: Princeton University Press.

Mills, J. P.
1926.   *The Ao Nagas.* London: Macmillan and Co.

Nugent, D.
1982.   "Closed System and Contradiction: The Kachin in and out of History." *Man* (N.S.) 17(3): 508-527.

Schulte Nordholt, H.
1971.   *The Political System of the Atoni of Timor.*   The Hague:
         Martinus Nijoff.

Stevenson, H.
1943.   *The Economics of the Central Chin Tribes.* London: Gregg.

CONTRIBUTORS

E. Paul Durrenberger is a professor in the Department of Anthropology, University of Iowa, Iowa City.

Frederic K. Lehman is a professor in the Department of Anthropology, University of Illinois, Urbana-Champaign.

Richard A. O'Connor is an associate professor in the Department of Anthropology, University of the South, Sewanee, Tennessee.

Susan D. Russell is an assistant professor in the Department of Anthropology, Northern Illinois University, DeKalb.

Nicola Tannenbaum is an assistant professor in the Department of Social Relations, Lehigh University, Pennsylvania.

Mark R. Woodward is an assistant professor in the Department of Religious Studies, Arizona State University, Tempe.

Occasional Paper Series

#13—E. Paul Durrenberger. *Lisu Religion.* 1989. 44pp. Figure. $7.00.

#12—Raymond Lee, editor. *Ethnicity and Ethnic Relations in Malaysia.* 1986. 178pp. Bibliography. $15.00

#11—John A. Lent and Kent Mulliner, editors. *Malaysian Studies: Archaeology, Historiography, Geography, and Bibliography.* 1985. 235pp. Bibliographies. $14.00

#10—Lawrence F. Ashmun. *Resettlement of Indochinese Refugees in the United States: A Selective and Annotated Bibliography.* 1983. 207pp. Indices (DAI; ERIC; RMC; subject). $14.00

#9—Penny Van Esterik, editor. *Women of Southeast Asia.* 1982. 279pp. Tables, figures, appendix, bibliography, index. **(Out-of-Print)**

#8—Donn V. Hart, editor. *Philippine Studies: Political Science, Economics, and Linguistics.* 1981. 285pp. Bibliographies, index. $14.00

#7—John A. Lent, editor. *Malaysian Studies: Present Knowledge and Research Trends.* 1979. 466pp. Charts, tables, bibliographies. **(Out-of-Print)**

#6—Donn V. Hart, editor. *Philippine Studies: History, Sociology, Mass Media and Bibliography.* 1978. 402pp. Charts, graphs, bibliographies, index. **(Out-of-Print)**

#5—Donn V. Hart. *Thailand: An Annotated Bibliography of Bibliographies.* 1977. 96pp. Index. $4.00

#4—Donn V. Hart. *An Annotated Bibliography of Philippine Bibliographies, 1965-1974.* 1974. 158pp. Index. $7.50

#3—Gerald S Marynov. *The Condition of Southeast Asian Studies in the United States: 1972.* In cooperation with the Southeast Asian Regional Council, The Association of Asian Studies. 1974. 68pp. Tables, bibliography. **(Out-of-Print)**

#2—Ronald L. Krannich, Herbert J. Rubin, Pratya Vesarach, and Chakrapand Wongburanavart. *Urbanization in Thailand.* Center for Governmental Studies, Northern Illinois University. 1974. 116pp. Bibliographies. **(Out-of-Print)**

#1—David W. Dellinger, editor. *Language, Literature, and Society: Working Papers from the 1973 Conference of American Council of Teachers of Uncommonly-Taught Asian Languages.* 1974. 85pp. Tables, charts. **(Out-of-Print)**

Special Report Series

#24—Robert Wessing. *The Soul of Ambiguity: The Tiger in Southeast Asia.* 1986. 148pp. Bibliography. $9.50

#23—Phil Scanlon, Jr. *Southeast Asia: A Cultural Study through Celebration.* 1985. 185pp. Photographs, index. $14.00

#22—David Hicks. *A Maternal Religion: The Role of Women in Tetum Myth and Ritual.* 1984. 146pp. Index, photographs. **(Out-of-Print)**

#21—Theodora Helene Bofman. *The Poetics of the Ramakian.* 1984. 258pp. Appendices, bibliography. $15.00

#20—Dwight Y. King. *Interest Groups and Political Linkage in Indonesia, 1800-1965.* 1982. 187pp. Bibliography, index. $12.50

#19—Robert J. Morais. *Social Relations in a Philippine Town.* 1981. 151pp. Tables, photographs, bibliography, index. $11.00

#18—Carol J. Compton. *Courting Poetry in Laos: A Textual and Linguistic Analysis.* 1979. 257pp. Photographs, charts, appendices, bibliography. **(Out-of-Print)**

#17—John B. Haseman. *The Thai Resistance Movement During the Second World War.* 1978. 192pp. Maps, charts, tables, bibliography, index. **(Out-of-Print)**

#16—George Vinal Smith. *The Dutch in Seventeenth Century Thailand.* 1977. 203pp. Maps, charts, tables, glossary, appendices, bibliography, index. **(Out-of-Print)**

#15—Michael M. Calavan. *Decisions Against Nature: An Anthropological Study of Agriculture in Northern Thailand.* 1977. 210pp. Maps, illustrations, charts, tables, bibliography, index. **(Out-of-Print)**

#14—John A. Lent, editor. *Cultural Pluralism in Malaysia: Polity, Military, Mass Media, Education, Religion and Social Class.* 1977. 114pp. Charts, tables, bibliography, index. **(Out-of-Print)**

#13—Douglas E. Foley. *Philippine Rural Education: An Anthropological Perspective.* 1976. 114pp. Table, bibliography, index. **(Out-of-Print)**

#12—G. N. Appell, editor. *Studies in Borneo Societies: Social Process and Anthropological Explanation.* 1976. 158pp. Maps, bibliography, index. **(Out-of-Print)**

#11—Howard M. Leichter. *Political Regime and Public Policy in the Philippines: A Comparison of Bacolod and Iloilo Cities.* 1975. 163pp. Bibliography, maps, charts, table, index. $4.00

#10—Fredrick Wernstedt, Wilhelm Solheim II, Lee Sechrest, George Guthrie, and Leonard Casper. *Philippine Studies: Geography, Archaeology, Psychology, and Literature: Present Knowledge and Research Trends.* 1974. 113pp. Annotated bibliography, index. **(Out-of-Print)**

#9—Harry Aveling. *A Thematic History of Indonesian Poetry: 1920-1974.* 1974. 90pp. Selected bibliography. **(Out-of-Print)**

#8—Herbert J. Rubin. *The Dynamics of Development in Rural Thailand.* 1974. 159pp. Maps, charts, tables. **(Out-of-Print)**

#7—Carl H. Landé with the assistance of Shirley Advincula, Augusto Ferreros, and James Frane. *Southern Tagalog Voting, 1946-1963: Political Behavior in a Philippine Region.* 1973. 159pp. Bibliography, index, maps. $4.00

#6—Richard L. Stone. *Philippine Urbanization: The Politics of Public and Private Property in Greater Manila.* 1973. 149pp. Bibliography, appendices. **(Out-of-Print)**

#5—David H. de Queljoe. *A Preliminary Study of Some Phonetic Features of Pentani, with Glossaries.* 1971. 114pp. Glossary. **(Out-of-Print)**

#4—Clark D. Neher. *Rural Thai Government: The Politics of the Budgetary Process.* 1970. 60pp. **(Out-of-Print)**

#3—Chan Ansuchote. *The 1969 General Elections in Thailand.* 1970. 44pp. **(Out-of-Print)**

#2—David H. de Queljoe. *A Preliminary Study of Malay/Indonesian Orthography.* 1969. 91pp. Bibliography. **(Out-of-Print)**

#1—J. A. Niels Mulder. *Monks, Merit, and Motivation: Buddhism and National Development in Thailand.* Second (revised and enlarged) edition. 1973. 58pp. (*Monks, Merit, and Motivation: An Exploratory Study of the Social Functions of Buddhism in Thailand in Processes of Guided Social Change.* 1961. 43pp.) **(Out-of-Print)**

Other Center Publications:

Donn V. Hart, compiler. *Theses and Dissertations on Southeast Asia Presented at Northern Illinois University, 1960-1980: An Annotated Bibliography.* Bibliographical Publication No. 6, 1980. 33pp. $3.00.

Richard M. Cooler. *British Romantic Views of the First Anglo-Burmese War, 1824-1826.* 1977. 41pp. $4.00.

AVAILABLE FROM:

The Cellar Book Shop

18090 Wyoming
Detroit, MI 48221
USA

Crossroads:
An Interdisciplinary Journal of Southeast Asian Studies

Back issues available at $6 per issue unless otherwise noted:

Volume 1, #1	Philippine Studies—Topical Issue (Out-of-Print)
Volume 1, #2	General Issue (Out-of-Print)
Volume 1, #3	Southeast Asian Studies and International Business (Out-of-Print)
Volume 2, #1	General Issue (Out-of-Print)
Volume 2, #2	Two Hundred Years of the Chakri Dynasty (Out-of-Print)
Volume 2, #3	General Issue
Volume 3, #1	Seven Hundred Years of Thai Writing
Volume 3, #2-3	General Issue
Volume 4, #1	Special Burma Issue ($8 for non-subscribers)

Forthcoming Issue:

Volume 4, #2	A Focus on Thailand

Subscriptions are available at $10 per year for two issues delivered at book rate. For air mail delivery, add cost of air mail postage for 12 oz. to destination per issue. Send subscription orders to: Center for Southeast Asian Studies, 140 Carroll Ave., Northern Illinois University, DeKalb, IL 60115. Checks should be made payable to the "Center for Southeast Asian Studies."

Also available from the Center:

The Twenty-fifth Anniversary of the Center for Southeast Asian Studies, Northern Illinois University, DeKalb, Illinois. 1988. 40pp. $2.00.

NOTES

NOTES